CONSCIOUS CHOICES

An Updated Version of *Authentic Spirituality*

OTHER BOOKS BY THE AUTHOR:

Soul Musings

Anatomy of Caring

A Caregiver's Journal

CONSCIOUS CHOICES

A Woman's Guide
to Clarity, Courage and Connection

CHRISTINE GREEN

Park Point Press | 573 Park Point Drive | Golden CO 80401

Conscious Choices:
A Woman's Guide to Clarity, Courage and Connection
Copyright © 2024, Christine Green
Originally published as *Authentic Spirituality*, Copyright © 2012

All rights reserved.
No part of this book may be reproduced in any form without permission
in writing from the publisher, except for brief quotations embodied in critical
articles or reviews.

Park Point Press
573 Park Point Drive
Golden, CO 80401-7402
720-496-1370

www.csl.org/publications/books
www.scienceofmind.com/publish-your-book

Printed in the United States of America
Published February 2024

Editor: Julie Mierau, JM Wordsmith
Design/Layout: Maria Robinson, Designs On You, LLC

ISBN paperback: 978-1-956198-31-7
ISBN ebook: 978-1-956198-32-4

To my sister, Joni

And to my spiritual sisters
who inspired me on this amazing journey

Advance Praise for *Conscious Choices*

Conscious Choices brilliantly, gently, and compassionately guides us through navigating the challenges of existing in time and space. Open the book to any page for inspiration, affirmations, and practices for expanding and evolving through the journey of life. An excellent resource for daily spiritual work, book clubs, or working with clients. Christine Green knows her stuff and knows how to share it in loving language that will touch your heart.

— J. ALISON HILBER, author,
I Am Who I Am: Sacredly Accepting My Body Temple

If you are open to transcendent guidance to move beyond your limiting beliefs and into the truth of your being, *Conscious Choices* is a trustworthy source. The vivid stories, transformative affirmations, prayers, and tested tools provided by Christine Green support the reader as they move into the wholeness they seek.

— GEORGENA GRACE, author,
A New Mourning: Discovering the Gifts in Grief

Christine Green has a gift for taking spiritual principles and giving them a very human face—the one we see in the mirror. Situations from her own life and the lives of her clients describe the predictable results that happen when habitual beliefs run amok. We are invited to examine how our own thinking (reinforced by our families, society, and culture) brings us to similar situations. From there, she guides us to the more productive path of self-acceptance, refreshed thinking, and generosity of spirit toward ourselves and others.

— LOUISE CARNACHAN, author,
Work Jerks: How to Cope with Difficult Bosses and Colleagues

Conscious Choices offers a well-grounded perspective on living a faith-filled life. Christine's writing is clear, friendly, and thoughtful, and she allows us to see her as a friend on her journey.

— LYNN SHERMAN, writer

This book is a useful, engaging tool that women will pick up over and over again to help move them along their life journey.

— REV. DEBORAH HOBBIE

I am forever grateful for Christine and her amazing book *Conscious Choices*. I was blessed to find both when I was going through a tough time, and I couldn't have felt more loved, guided, empowered, and understood. This book inspires readers with love, wisdom, joy, and humor, and gives readers life-changing tools and spiritual practices to use that uplift, enlighten, and heal. This timeless, loving guide is a must-read for every woman.

— TERI PRINCE
Centers for Spiritual Living Practitioner/Spiritual Coach

Christine Green offers a clear, compassionate, and useful guide to intimacy in the most fundamental relationship —the relationship with oneself. This book is an ideal companion for anyone exploring what it means to live a conscious and authentic life.

— BARBARA BUCKINGHAM HAYES
Centers for Spiritual Living Practitioner

Contents

Foreword x

Preface xii

Introduction xiv

1. Becoming the Observer 1

2. Would You Say that to Your Best Friend? 19

3. Kick Doubt Out! 37

4. Leave Your Victim Self Behind 57

5. This, Too, Shall Pass 75

6. Money Talks—Are You Listening? 93

7. Hanging on May Be Hazardous to Your Health ... 115

8. You Don't Have to Be Nice to Be Good 131

9. Looking for Love in All the Wrong Places 147

10. Living by Faith 163

Chapter Overview 182

Study Guide 184

About the Author 190

Foreword

CONSCIOUS CHOICES is a book written by a woman who knows the path of deep spiritual awakening and full self-expression.

I met Christine in 1980, long before either of us knew we would be ministers. She was working for a high-profile and rapidly growing ministry, and as part of my taking the first steps on the spiritual journey, I became her volunteer. Christine was then, as she is now, bright and beautiful. She was always kind and tolerant when I brought my one-year-old son to the ministry office so he could play at my feet while I worked.

I began to assist her on Sundays in Children's Church, and as the years progressed, our spirituality unfolded, and our friendship deepened. I opened a church where Christine was a beloved leader, licensed practitioner, and board president. Through those years, we grew up all over each other, rubbed off our rough corners on each other, and served as mutual agents of awakening. While I stayed in San Diego, life took Christine to the Pacific Northwest, where she began her ministry. Our paths crossed periodically, and our heartfelt connection remained.

And so, it is my delight to read this book and to witness the profound wisdom of a sister, friend, and colleague who has been an important part of my own

Foreword

transformative journey. Christine has walked her path with unfaltering devotion and commitment to seeing clearly and understanding deeply the inner side of her own human challenges and conditions. Such resoluteness allowed her to arrive at spiritual realizations and solutions that are the way out of limitation and fear.

Because she walked her own walk with consciousness and intention, she now can share her insights and guidance with others. Each chapter of this book offers clear perceptions and an acute articulation of important topics. Her writing on transcending victim mentality, forgiveness, and taking responsibility for creating our own happiness is some of the best I have ever read on these subjects. She illuminates spiritual principles in a way that opens the doors of realization. She offers practices that anchor those realizations in practical living.

What *Conscious Choices* makes available to the reader is the experience of daily life, with all of its "interesting and challenging aspects, as a spiritual adventure that ultimately leads to joy and fulfillment.

There is much to appreciate here. Open your heart and mind and choose a chapter that speaks to what you are working on in your life. You and your world will be the better for it.

— REV. KATHY HEARN

Dean, San Diego Campus, School of Spiritual Leadership

Preface

*It is literally impossible to be a woman.
You are so beautiful, and so smart, and it kills me
that you don't think you're good enough.
Like, we have to always be extraordinary, but somehow
we're always doing it wrong.*

— GLORIA, *BARBIE* (THE MOVIE)

BELIEVING WE ARE NOT GOOD enough is our deepest secret. Women are trained to keep our secrets and pain to ourselves. *Don't air your dirty laundry. Don't complain to others. Keep your problems to yourself.* As a result, we tend to think we are alone and are the only ones dealing with doubt, self-judgment, and lack.

The truth is we do our best work when we share with others. Over the years of teaching and counseling, I watched women blossom as they engage and connect with others. We are wired to communicate and commiserate with others. It makes all the difference to know we are not alone and to confide in a trusted friend in a safe space, sharing our worries, pain, desires, and dreams.

Since the time *Authentic Spirituality* was published in 2012, I have facilitated a variety of study groups, workshops, and retreats and have been delighted with how the book served as a catalyst for growth and change.

Preface

Readers shared how the stories in the book speak to the issues they were dealing with daily.

We live in a changing and challenging time. Anxiety, stress, and loneliness are reported to be at the highest levels. Our decisions and choices impact our families and us in ways we could not have imagined a few years ago. We are being called to live in a more expansive consciousness, which inspired me to change the name of this book to *Conscious Choices: A Woman's Guide to Clarity, Courage and Connection*. When our intention is to make conscious choices, we open to greater clarity, which gives us the courage to move forward. With clarity and courage, we experience a greater connection with ourselves and our oneness with Spirit.

The chapters in this edition have been updated and revised. There is a study guide for anyone inspired to facilitate their own group. You can access free worksheets to dive deeper into your spiritual practice at www.revchristine.com/books.

I would love to hear how you are able to put the principles into practice. Please reach out to me through my website, www.revchristine.com/contact-revchristine/. Thank you for allowing me to part of your spiritual journey.

With Gratitude,
Christine

Introduction

*When change-winds swirl through our lives,
they often call us to undertake a new passage of the
spiritual journey: that of confronting the lost and
counterfeit places within us and releasing our deeper,
innermost self—our true self. They call us to come home
to ourselves, to become who we really are.*

— SUE MONK KIDD, *When the Heart Waits*

MY FIRST CRISIS OF FAITH happened around age ten. Sister Mary announced to our class that if you did not confess your sins, when you died, you would go to purgatory. It wasn't heaven, and it wasn't hell; it was a place of nothing, an eternal place of being on hold.

Now, I was a good Catholic girl. I attended Catholic School for nine years. I went to mass every Sunday, as well as to confession, whether I thought I had sinned or not.

The idea of purgatory—where I wouldn't see my loved ones, or Jesus, or God—was overwhelming. I couldn't think of any greater punishment than that. If God really loved me, then why would he send me to this awful place of nothingness? How does one get out of purgatory? How long is eternity?

Introduction

I remember asking these and other questions that were swirling in my head—out loud. The answers from the nuns were always the same: "That's just the way it is. It is a mystery. We can't understand it here on Earth, but we will when we are in heaven." But what if I'm stuck in purgatory? Does no one understand my dilemma? Please! I need some answers!

My turmoil over spending eternity in purgatory eventually got pushed aside as the years went by. There were football games, school dances, first loves, broken hearts, and many more important issues to cope with. As a teenager, I was out late one Saturday night and didn't want to go to church the next day. My father's response was unyielding: "If you live in this house, you will go to church." That moment cleared up everything for me. This was my parents' religion. I would find my own answers to my questions.

As soon as I left home, I stopped going to Sunday mass—and church—altogether. I still believed in God, and I was not going to feel guilty about my life. I faced a crucial choice that would forever change my relationship with God. In that moment, I chose to explore my inner experience of God and my authentic expression.

There are many paths to connecting with God, and each of us is called in our own unique direction. Authentic is defined as genuine, original, real. Authentic spirituality is a quest to discover a deeper understanding of ourselves in relationship with our divinity.

Many of us leave the religion of our childhood to find the meaning and value of our souls. It is a courageous step to let go of that security and to venture out on our personal quest. Change can feel more daunting than the desire to be authentic.

My studies over the past twenty years brought me to a place of peace with the teachings I learned from Catholicism and to an even deeper connection with God and my faith. My spiritual quest brought me to a better understanding of what I believe. My journey led me to a greater understanding of my faith. I found a place to be authentic.

In my work as an ordained minister and spiritual mentor, I have the privilege of working with strong, powerful, courageous women who are on their own spiritual journeys, discovering their authentic selves. I discovered, both from my own journey and from witnessing others, that once we can get past our pain, frustration, and challenges, we have an experience of exquisite joy and freedom in life. As we learn to take ourselves more lightly, we can approach the difficult challenges with grace.

My vision for this book is to reveal an inspired pathway to love. I share lessons I learned, along with lessons I observed in others. The spiritual practice section provided at the end of each chapter includes practices I have successfully used to let go of old beliefs and to transform challenges into blessings. I have cleaned out my share of limiting beliefs: *I can't have what I want. There is not enough.*

Introduction

I am unworthy. I came back from near bankruptcy and paid off my $20,000 debt in full. Over the years, I struggled to find a job I liked and, in the process, discovered my ministry. I faced my fears of being alone and met my amazing husband.

This book is a guide to releasing the beliefs that clutter our thinking. It is an invitation to pull out old beliefs, observe them, and, like an old pair of jeans, try them on one last time. Then it's time to toss them out. Nature abhors a vacuum, so it is a good idea to replace the old beliefs with something that empowers and supports us. Spiritual principles give us a new way to look at life.

Chapter One sets the tone for becoming an observer. The practice at the end of the chapter is a great tool to help jumpstart your journaling.

Chapters Two through Nine identify the beliefs that keep us stuck and the emotions that clutter our thinking. It's not necessary to read them in the order they appear here. Instead, find the chapter that relates to the belief that keeps you stuck. If relationship issues are driving you crazy, read Chapter Nine. When you are trapped in victim thinking, read Chapter Four. If money or a lack of money keeps you awake at night, read Chapter Six. (There is a summary overview of the chapters at the end of this book.)

Chapter Ten completes the process by reminding us of the blessings of faith and of the importance of living in Divine Oneness.

Use the affirmations sprinkled throughout the chapters to help shift your thinking. The spiritual practice at the end of each chapter helps guide the healing process and quiet the noise of the pesky inner critic. Each practice also will support you in releasing the old patterns of thinking and the emotional roller coaster that accompanies them.

Use the prayers to anchor your faith. There are many names for God: Spirit, Universe, Divinity, Love, Creative Expression, Source, Infinite, etc. Rewrite the prayers and use the name that works for you. Post the prayers on your bathroom mirror. Read them out loud. Make them your own.

Be sure to download the chapter worksheets at www.revchristine.com/books. They are provided to support your awareness and growth.

There is a study guide in the back of the book to use if you are interested in hosting a study group. Be sure to sign up for my mailing list and let me know if you are interested in attending a training for study group facilitators.

The spiritual journey is not necessarily an easy one. On this journey, we are called to lay down our beliefs, our limitations, and our fears. The effort takes willingness, patience, and a mountain of faith. The rewards, however, are priceless and enduring.

Blessings to you on your journey.

CONSCIOUS CHOICES

A Woman's Guide
to Clarity, Courage and Connection

CHAPTER 1

Becoming the Observer

The unexamined life is not worth living.

— SOCRATES

OBSERVING THE SELF BEGINS with being aware of the inner critic, that pesky voice that kicks us when we are down, criticizes us when we feel low, and nags us when we want to rest. Speaking from old beliefs and ideas, the critic can knock us down with a whisper. The key to having more mastery of our lives is to be conscious of what we hear and more discerning about what we believe.

In her book, *You Can Heal Your Life,* Louise Hay teaches us that regardless of the problem, the situations we face are a result of our inner thoughts. The inner thought produces an emotion and we attach ourselves to the emotion. The more mindful we are of our thoughts, the sooner we can acknowledge them, change them, and be set free.

While we can't see our beliefs, our emotions are indicators that they are there. Someone who pushes our buttons is a great teacher and gives us the opportunity to practice being the observer. When we take responsibility for our emotions and don't blame or judge ourselves—or others—we can be set free.

I learned firsthand how important taking responsibility was.

My new job was class registrar at my church. Linda was my supervisor and trained me in my new position. I was convinced that Linda relished the opportunity to tell me what to do, what not to do, when to do it, and how to do it better. She was quick to bring my mistakes to my attention and was an expert at clarifying how to correct them. She was obsessive about details and committed to perfection.

Linda quickly became my nemesis. I grumbled about Linda every night when I went home. I thought about how she controlled me, nagged me, and just made my life miserable. I was suffering, and I knew Linda was the cause. Even when I was away from the office, she haunted my thoughts and emotions.

Later that year, I enrolled in an eight-week spiritual growth class. During this class, I learned that I would feel much more peaceful if I quit blaming Linda and took responsibility for my life. I learned to become the observer of life and not the victim. I discovered that I could become aware of my emotions and choose how to respond to the situation.

Linda pushed my buttons, and I felt like a victim. When I did my spiritual work and observed my feelings, I recognized an inner belief that said, "I am not enough." By identifying that belief, I was able to withdraw my projections against Linda and take responsibility for how

I was feeling. Linda no longer pushed my buttons and, over time, became a trusted friend.

Running away from whatever causes us pain without looking at the cause is fruitless. The same irritating behavior we are trying to escape will show up again as a different person, a different time, a different place, but it will cause the same reaction. Imagine the freedom we would have if we did not run away from people who pushed our buttons and instead had the compassion and awareness to know that they were not responsible for our pain. The belief behind the emotion is the culprit.

<blockquote>
AFFIRM:
I am willing to accept responsibility
for my emotions.
</blockquote>

Being the observer is not for the tender-hearted. It demands looking within and being willing to surrender. Is it worth the journey? You bet it is! What is waiting on the other side is the gift of extraordinary freedom. What it takes is discipline, patience, and humility.

Discipline

EXCUSES ARE EASY: *I don't have time. I don't feel like it. It won't make any difference.* Discipline is tough. Any new practice or new behavior demands discipline.

The word "disciple" comes from the Latin, meaning, "to learn." A disciple is one dedicated and committed to the work. As disciples, we have faith that what we are doing is making a difference in our lives.

Volumes have been written about changing behavior, getting results, and moving forward. The critical component is discipline. Nike says it best with their slogan, "Just do it."

We are each unique. We each have our own perception of life, patterns of behavior, and activities we are passionate about. Likewise, there is no one-size-fits-all remedy to resolve the resistance to change and to move forward. There are, however, guidelines that are beneficial to anyone committed to a spiritual discipline.

A simple technique embraced in the Japanese culture to achieve change is called kaizen. It is the practice of implementing change by taking tiny steps toward the new behavior that we want to embody. Author Robert Maurer shares an experience in his book *One Small Step Can Change Your Life*. His client said that her doctor advised her to exercise for thirty minutes each day, but she just couldn't seem to follow this schedule. Maurer suggested that instead she start by marching in place in front of the television every day for one minute. By reducing the new behavior to a small activity, the mind finds it doable and is willing to cooperate. This practice supported his client into moving from one minute a day to eventually increasing her exercise time to the goal of thirty minutes daily.

AFFIRM:
I am energized to take action.

On the spiritual journey we often believe we have to devote hours to meditation, journaling, prayer, and spiritual practices. While that may work for some, I suggest picking one new practice you want to incorporate and spending ten minutes practicing. By taking a small step toward change, i.e. ten minutes, we experience a win and are encouraged to take another small step and then another. This process allows us to make more solid progress toward actual change. The most important step is taking action. Commit to your practice.

How do we build on discipline? Patience.

Patience

HOW MUCH TIME DOES IT TAKE to change? Time can seem to take forever when we're waiting. However, it takes an instant when we release our attachment to the results. Time moves so slowly when we don't like our circumstances. Yet time seems to fly by when we are expressing our talents in life. Change is always occurring, even when we aren't aware of it, just not always on our time schedule.

AFFIRM:
I patiently practice.

George Leonard shares in his book *Mastery* that in martial arts training there comes a time when it appears the student is no longer improving. The student appears stagnant and stuck at a particular skill level. In fact, there is considerable activity of the spirit, mind, body, and soul all coming into alignment. The challenge is to not stop practicing but to continue regardless of the external results. Progress is happening on an inner level that we can't see. The gift of patience is the development of our faith. Faith is believing that in spite of current conditions, change for the better will occur.

We are addicted to the quick fix, the microwave answer. One of the first questions I commonly hear in my mentoring program is: How long will this [desired change] take? My response is always the same: How much are you willing to practice? We often avoid looking at our limitations for as long as possible, until the pain is too much to take and we want it to end. If we want out of the pain, we must make the effort to change. It may take time to unravel our old ideas, but once we incorporate uplifted ideas, the change we desire is revealed.

The universe is proceeding with perfect timing;
if you believe it is not,
it is not an error in the universe,
but in your perception.
— ALLAN COHEN

The ego wants to see results. The spiritual journey takes patience and commitment. Waiting comes from hope. We hope something will happen, but there is a part of us that doubts. So we wait, expecting something to change. Patience comes from faith. We have faith that what we ask for is already realized. We have faith that the change we want will come. When practicing patience, it helps to have compassion for ourselves.

Compassion

WE LIVE IN A SOCIETY that places a high value on validating the ego. We take a lot of pride in what we accomplish, and those accomplishments become part of our identity. As we observe this ego-based identity within ourselves, we find our weaknesses and limitations. Our self-esteem takes a hit, and it is tempting to slide back into old ways of thinking.

However, it is important for us to recognize that our worth is not defined by our accomplishments or our ego. Our self-worth comes from within, from our intrinsic value as human beings. It is OK to fail and to make mistakes, as long as we learn from them and grow.

Buddha taught the importance of having compassion for ourselves before we can have it for others: "It is possible to travel the whole world in search of one who is more worthy of compassion than oneself. No such person can be found."

Unless we have compassion for ourselves, we can easily be pulled into wanting to be better than everyone else. What is hidden in the unconscious is the fear of feeling inferior. When times are tough, we feel the pressure of being high functioning, so we scramble to hold things together. This becomes a vicious cycle, as we puff ourselves up and try to hide any weakness or flaw. There is little room for compassion in the race to the top.

Consider Regina's story:

> Regina was top sales producer in the region. Her job was highly competitive and so was the top producer spot. Regina was bold, brash, and con-

fident, but the fight for the top spot took its toll on her. Anxiety medications helped calm her nerves. Another pill helped her sleep, and energy drinks helped her stay alert all day. She suppressed her fears of missing her goal and of making mistakes. She defined herself by her work. The thought of losing it terrified her.

Women performing in highly competitive jobs often lose their sense of self as they suppress their fears and vulnerability to stay strong and competent in the working world. The fear of making mistakes can be crippling. Identifying errors, mistakes, or faults can be extremely painful if we wed our self-worth to our accomplishments.

As we are compassionate with ourselves, we learn not to judge each mistake but instead view each one as an opportunity to grow. Observing our errors becomes less threatening and more inspiring as we adopt new ways of thinking. We experience empathy for ourselves as we become aware of our spiritual journey.

AFFIRM:
I observe myself with compassion.

When we step out of the ego and look at the gifts of our talents and abilities, we feel humbled. Consider the life of Rev. Robert, a minister who asked God in his prayer to show him which of his gifts came from God and which came from his own efforts. Within a week, Rev. Robert lost his ability to write, speak, and teach. A short time later, he lost his voice and movement. He quickly came to realize that all his talents came from God. It was a humbling but powerful revelation.

Compassion helps us put life into perspective. It allows us to step back from the frenetic energy of the world and step into the internal chamber of peace. Discipline, patience, and compassion are helpful strengths to have in order to change.

Spiritual Principle:
Change My Thinking, Change My Life

OUR PERCEPTION OF LIFE determines how we deal with our day-to-day encounters. Do we experience life as the victim or the student? The victim blames others, is powerless, and lives at the effect of emotions. The student observes the situation, takes responsibility, and gleans a lesson from the experience. The victim asks, "Why did this happen to me?" The student asks, "What can I learn from this experience?" We begin by changing our thinking.

I've researched, examined, and explored, and I discovered that there is no secret mantra that will make change easier. I also discovered that no one can change my thinking for me. I became ready to change when I noticed that I had a limited belief that there was never enough. Not enough time, energy, money, ideas, people. I heard myself repeating the same limited thinking and excuses. I knew I was ready and willing to do the work. There had to be a better life than what I was experiencing.

Chapter 1 — Becoming the Observer

*Thoughts are things and occupy space in the mind.
We cannot have new or better ones
in a place already crowded
with old, weak, inefficient thoughts.*

— CHARLES FILLMORE

A quality life takes conscious attention to focus and a willingness to look deep within. There is an opportunity for greater peace when we are aware of our emotional being and consciously move into the expression of our true spiritual self. We have to be willing to take dominion over our lives. We make a choice to step into the spiritual journey.

Some of the essential tools for the journey include meditating, journaling, taking personal growth classes, reading inspirational materials, praying, connecting with a mentor or prayer counselor, and embracing other practices that raise our vibration. Effectively using these tools takes practice, discipline, and patience. They train us in being mindful and developing greater awareness.

AFFIRM:
Awareness of myself brings peace.

Writing in a journal provides the opportunity to act as observer and witness to our life experiences. The writing practice at the end of this chapter helps to separate facts from beliefs. By stepping outside of ourselves, we can identify our limiting beliefs and thoughts that keep repeating throughout our lives. The practice of writing in my journal about my suffering from limiting thinking and emotional turmoil was the catalyst for me to change my thinking, my behavior, and my circumstances.

I find that women often are hesitant to write down their deepest thoughts for fear that someone will find and read them. Keep your journal in a safe place. It is important to make the journaling practice comfortable so you then can make it consistent. Your spiritual practice is not secret but sacred. Journaling is a personal practice meant to help us deepen in our own awareness. As with anything sacred, we keep it close to the heart.

In meditation, we practice mindfulness, which allows us to be the onlooker of our thoughts and to gently allow them to pass on by. Mindfulness is simple but not easy. When I began meditating, my experience of constant mind chatter frustrated me. I was shocked when I realized how much inner noise lives in my mind. It takes patience and persistence to bring your mind to a place of quiet. When the mind chatter finally settles, we experience calmness, peace, and a connection with our divine oneness.

To live a life of conscious awareness, we learn to be aware of emotions and behaviors. We learn to be less reactive and find more balance. We have more compassion for ourselves and others. Instead of struggling with the diverse challenges and responsibilities of life, we identify the common thread of beliefs and have a deeper understanding with greater peace. Instead of being reactive to the world, we can take dominion of our lives.

Chapter 1 — Becoming the Observer

*Nothing can bring you peace but yourself.
Nothing can bring you peace but the triumph of principles.*

— RALPH WALDO EMERSON

In the absence of reaction to ordinary experiences, we find a presence of peace that opens us to a greater experience of Spirit. As I moved into my inner awareness through meditation, prayer, and journaling, I became aware of the universal qualities of God, such as love, peace, joy, beauty, and abundance. These qualities of life are freeing and connect us with our spiritual nature and with the universal flow. The qualities are expansive rather than restrictive. They bring more freedom to our daily living.

Living in the Pacific Northwest, I have the blessing of hiking in the nearby forest. I am continually in awe of the exquisite beauty that surrounds me. Walking on the Oregon coast and observing the tremendous energy of the ocean, I am taken with the unlimited power of nature. I experience gentle peace when I sit in meditation. I recognize Spirit is everywhere and in every moment. As we train ourselves to be observers, we can more easily connect with the universal qualities that surround us.

As we become aware of our beliefs, we are free to take responsibility for them and change our thinking and the circumstances of our lives. As we think new thoughts, we deepen in our faith.

Eric Butterworth reminds us, "When you turn within, centering your attention on God, the center and source of being, there will come a moment of faith's fruition, and that which you perceive inwardly you will soon be seeing the light of day."

The spiritual journey is simple but not easy. The benefits are peace of mind, creative expression, and living a grace-filled life. Get ready to observe your new life.

Chapter 1 — Becoming the Observer

Prayer for Joyful Acceptance

As I look out at the beauty around me,

I recognize an Infinite Creative Power for all life.

I walk in peace, knowing I am guided

and directed along my spiritual journey.

I accept patience, courage,

and faith as my travel companions.

I approach this day with joy in my heart and

peace in my mind, knowing that wisdom guides

my path and lights my way.

I am so grateful for

recognizing these gracious blessings.

And so it is.

SPIRITUAL PRACTICE

Conscious Journaling Technique

Journaling is the practice of recording our thoughts and feelings. Conscious journaling is recording our thoughts with the intention of seeing the higher good that emerges from the details.

Here are the steps I recommend for journaling:

(1) State the facts.
  - Act as a reporter. Record the who, what, where, and when of the event.

(2) Identify your feelings.
  - How does this event/experience make me feel?

(3) What do you believe?
  - What decisions am I making as a result of this event?

(4) Identify where or if this belief has shown up in the past.
  - When have I felt this way before?

(5) What is the new statement of affirmation you would like to make for yourself?
  - I am lovable and capable.
  - I am a loving communicator.
  - I experience peace in all activities.

<u>Example:</u>

I ran into Sally today, and she told me she had booked two new workshops and was invited to be the keynote speaker at a conference in Florida next month. I felt jealous because things have been quiet for me lately. Then I felt guilty because I couldn't feel happy for her. When I feel like this, I believe I'm not good enough to do this work. This is the nagging voice I hear so often. I have heard it so many times in the past when I compare myself to others. I am not going to let it get to me this time.

- I am grateful for my speaking talents.
- I am capable of leading successful workshops and presentations.
- I experience love and joy in my work and with my friends.

Download the chapter worksheet at
www.revchristine.com/books.

CHAPTER 2

Would You Say that to Your Best Friend?

The curious paradox is that when I accept myself just as I am, then I can change.

— CARL ROGERS

SELF-JUDGMENT is a particularly painful pastime for women. We judge ourselves with outdated beliefs and messages. Our inner critic constantly badgers us with "should" and "have to." Not to mention the frequent reminders: You can't have what you want. You're not good enough. How on Earth do you think you can pull that off?

> I was on my fourth outfit. Nothing seemed to look right. My husband, Laurence, patiently watched me and then said, "I wish you could see what I see and recognize how beautiful you are."
>
> "That's so sweet of you to say," I said, while thinking to myself, "How can he be so blind not to notice that nothing fits right? He can't possibly be serious. He's just saying that to be nice and get me out of the house."

A few days later, I was with a friend who was obsessing about her looks. While watching her, I suddenly understood what Laurence had been saying to me. I saw how beautiful she looked inside and out. I recognized her inner beauty and outer strength.

Our internal critic is compounded with the barrage of society's messages about how we look, what we wear, what products we use, or which handbag we carry. Corporate advertisers find the weakest link in our self-esteem and prey on that fear with aggressive advertising. Our rational mind knows that photos are airbrushed, retouched, and superimposed onto a fake backdrop. But it doesn't matter. We continue to judge and evaluate ourselves based on these false images.

AFFIRM:
My self-talk is loving and compassionate.

"The Real Truth about Beauty" was a global study that inspired The Dove Campaign for Real Beauty. Research showed that women around the world believed that the definition of beauty had become limiting and unattainable. Of the women responding to the survey, only 2 percent described themselves as beautiful. In the United States, 81 percent of the women agreed that "the media and advertising set an unrealistic standard of beauty that most women can never achieve."

Stephanie was 38 years old. She looked like she stepped off the cover of a magazine in her designer jeans, knee-length boots, and leather coat. She sat down in the chair in my office and started to weep. Her husband had recently ended their marriage. She confessed she felt unattractive and couldn't imagine anyone ever wanting to be in relationship with her again.

We spend so much time judging ourselves that we become prisoners of negative thinking. We judge our outer looks as being too big, too fat, too tall, too short, too anything. We believe we are not smart enough, capable enough, or qualified enough. While we are busy judging ourselves, we don't take time to appreciate the abundant blessings our lives have to offer.

Would you repeat the inner judgments you say to and about yourself to someone you loved? We wouldn't think of it. Yet, we beat ourselves up mentally and verbally until we are left exhausted, powerless, and immobilized. Self-criticism and judgment are debilitating habits. They break down our faith, erode our self-esteem, and stir up our feelings of shame.

Shame

SHAME IS A POWERFUL EMOTION that can make us feel powerless and isolated. When we are shamed, we feel like we have failed to meet the expectations placed on us by society, our family, or our friends. These expectations often are unattainable, complex, and conflicting, leaving us feeling overwhelmed and helpless. We may not even be aware of how much these expectations influence our behavior and our sense of self-worth. We may internalize these expectations, believing that we are not good enough, smart enough, or successful enough to meet them.

This internalized shame can have a profound impact on our lives. It can limit our potential, prevent us from taking risks, and make us feel like we are not deserving of love and respect. It can also lead to feelings of anxiety, depression, and other mental health issues.

AFFIRM:
I love my body. I love all that I see in me.

It's no wonder feelings of shame haunt us and contribute to a low self-image. We often believe we have failed to live up to the image impressed on us in childhood by well-meaning adults. As a result, we judge ourselves and feel unworthy and unlovable. The feeling of unworthiness can be an isolating experience that makes us believe we are completely alone and unique. In fact, the experience is so real that it shapes how we imagine others see us: No one could be as unlovable as I am. No one could want to like me.

> I remember when I first became aware of feeling unlovable.
>
> Getting braces on my teeth was a traumatic experience. I hated how they looked and how they felt. I was certain that people took one look and ran the other way on seeing my metal smile. I was already shy. Now with this handicap, I was sure to be friendless forever. I was extremely anxious when I met my potential new friend Cindy

at school and didn't want her to run away from my freakish appearance. I wanted to give her a reason to stay around, and so I actually said, "I hope you like me better next week when I get my braces off."

Author Brené Brown, Ph.D., author of *Women & Shame: Reaching Out, Speaking Truths and Building Connection*, uses this definition in her work: "Shame is the intensely painful feeling or experience of believing we are flawed and therefore unworthy of acceptance and belonging." Shame makes us feel as if others can see right through us and are judging us. In fact, it becomes the perception of how we view the world. An innocent comment, a prolonged stare, or a simple question can cause tremendous emotional pain if we focus on inner beliefs and perceptions of shame. In reality, we are usually far more self-critical and judgmental than anyone around us.

As children, we instinctively try to conform to our family dynamics in an effort to belong or be loved. We attach ourselves to the views and ideals of the adults around us. We strive to make them happy and try to live up to their expectations. It's difficult to break that habit as an adult.

As a result, we tend to apologize for our clumsy behavior or uneducated remarks before anyone else has the chance to speak up. What appears to be a harmless self-deprecating remark is internally a way to hide our shame and internal accusations.

We experience shame when we haven't lived up to the expectations of those around us. How else can we know how we are doing except to compare ourselves to others?

Comparison

ALL TOO OFTEN, WE COMPARE ourselves to others and make snap judgments based on our limited perceptions. While we know very little about the other person's life, we tend to make assumptions about what they can and cannot do. Our perception is often that they are more successful than we are. However, this way of comparing ourselves is not only unfair, but it is also inaccurate. We do not have all the information about the other person's journey, and we don't know the struggles, challenges, and setbacks they may have faced along the way. It is important to remember that every individual has their own unique path to follow, and their success cannot be measured by the same yardstick as our own.

In truth, we believe we don't meet our own standards. We tend to spend more time finding fault rather than acknowledging our strengths and accomplishments. I noticed my own feelings of comparing and competing when I ran into a friend.

> I bumped into a friend I hadn't seen in a while and hardly recognized her. She was at least twenty pounds lighter, had a new haircut, and looked fabulous. She was so excited that her new company was a success, and she had bookings for the next six months. I congratulated her on her success and hard work.

I walked away and immediately began to analyze how my life compared to hers. Why wasn't I at the same place that she was? Why haven't I progressed farther than I have? Why was I having difficulty achieving my goals? Why am I feeling that I'm not enough?

Before the conversation, I was happy with my life and content with the goals I set for myself. The moment I compared my life to hers, I felt anxious and inadequate. My accomplishments were diminished in light of her success.

When beauty pageants became popular in the early 1920s, women competed against other women to see who was the most beautiful. The first beauty pageant started as a gimmick by the owner of an Atlantic City hotel. He held the pageant to find the "most beautiful bathing beauty in America," but wanted the attention for his hotel. His marketing gimmick set superficial standards for women to compare and compete, pitting us against each other to be crowned a "winner."

AFFIRM:
My inner beauty radiates out as health, happiness, and joy.

Advertisers bombard us with unrealistic views of body types. We try so hard to measure up to the standards we see around us. We want to fit in, so we compare ourselves to others to see how we measure up. If we look deeper within ourselves, we realize we are judging more than just the body or celebrity image, but the symbols they represent. We inaccurately equate beauty with success, love, happiness, and living a fairytale life.

Rather than comparing ourselves to others, it is more important to focus on our own growth and progress. It is to our benefit to set our own goals and work toward achieving them, regardless of how long it takes or where we start from. Our only competition should be with ourselves—to be better than we were yesterday and to keep striving toward self-improvement.

There should be a warning label tattooed on our foreheads: Comparison can be hazardous to your health.

> *The body is a sacred garment.*
> *It's your first and last garment; it is what you*
> *enter life in and what you depart life with,*
> *and it should be treated with honor.*
>
> — MARTHA GRAHAM

When do we finally feel we are truly good enough? Sadly, when we are showered with praise and admiration from others. We can be addicted to acknowledgement.

Need for Acknowledgement

WE ALL WANT TO BE loved and respected. That need becomes a challenge when it becomes necessary to receive praise from others for self-validation, to believe that we are worthy and lovable. I remember when I wanted acknowledgement from my parents.

When I was growing up, our next-door-neighbor Bruce would talk constantly about his kids. He always talked about Catherine and Peter and how smart, creative, intelligent, high achieving, and all-around good kids they were. They could do nothing wrong. This kind of talk irritated my parents. They believed it was not OK to brag and be boastful. My parents were quiet, shy, and humble. They would never dream of carrying on like neighbor Bruce.

Not only was I jealous, I wanted my parents to be proud and to boast about my accomplishments and to sing my praises. Isn't that what we all want, to be acknowledged and to be loved?

But what happens when we aren't given the validation that we crave? We may feel lost, lonely, and worthless. Our self-esteem may plummet, and anxiety and depression may set in. The problem with seeking validation from external sources is that we put the power of our happiness and worthiness in the hands of others.

All too often, the people we want the praise and attention from are busy with their own issues of low self-esteem and unworthiness. I have noticed how many times over the years I have given my power away to someone who was buried too deep in their own process to even notice me.

To break free from this cycle, we must find validation within ourselves. Realizing our own self-worth and finding validation in our own accomplishments and self-love can be difficult, but it is crucial for our happiness and well-being. How rewarding would it be to be our own cheerleaders and find satisfaction in our own personal victories?

Seeking validation from external sources may provide temporary satisfaction, but true validation comes from within. We must learn to love and accept ourselves for who we are, flaws and all, in order to live fulfilled and happy lives.

Spiritual Principle:
Whatever I think about, I become.

EACH OF US IS A DIVINE BEING filled with beauty, love, and light. We are extraordinary individuals with unique talents, gifts, and abilities. Each of us has overcome obstacles, tackled tough problems, and accomplished courageous deeds. It's up to us to acknowledge ourselves.

It takes practice to be our own best friend and praise the good we've done. The more we focus on the good we see in ourselves, the more opportunities we attract and the more we deepen our positive self-esteem.

> Nicole had a revelation at work. She noticed that when someone asked her how to proceed with a project she would reply, "I have no idea what I am doing." If she was asked how she accomplished a task, she would state, "I have no clue how that came about." She realized one day that her comments were self-criticisms and a lie. Once she realized this, instead of saying she didn't know how to move forward, her new response was, "This is a new process for me, so I'm going to work from this angle." Instead of confessing to being clueless, she would affirm, "It's a process of inspiration and patience." This

new way of speaking became her springboard away from her constant self-judgment.

Nicole was able to break the cycle of self-criticism. Whatever standards she was attempting to live up to were reprogrammed to be more supportive and uplifting for her. She was able to move beyond the inflexible requirements of the past.

AFFIRM:
I consciously find new and exciting
ways to see my world.

Eve Einsler, author of *The Vagina Monologues*, reminds us that the need for the perfect body has been programmed into us since birth. Our preoccupation with diet, cosmetic surgery, and constant worrying about our looks is self-imposed. She goes on to call for women to skip their botox appointment, plastic surgery, and liposuction, and use that money to support women in other countries who don't have the freedom to speak out, get an education, or even have enough food to eat. She calls for us to lay down our obsession with the perfect body.

It's time to take dominion over how we see and think about ourselves. It's time to speak about ourselves with patience, compassion, and respect.

Taking responsibility shifts us out of blame and victimization. Blame does nothing to solve a problem or enhance our experience of life. I observed that the more I blamed, the farther love moved away from me. I notice that my energy is drained when I criticize and judge myself. Doubt, confusion, and limitation caused by judgment causes us to waste precious time and energy.

AFFIRM:
I am whole, perfect, and complete
just as I am.

Author Tara Brach, in her book *Radical Acceptance: Embracing Your Life with the Heart of a Buddha*, invites us to engage in radical acceptance by releasing our stories from the past and holding our current experience with vulnerability and compassion. As we do, we shift away from self-loathing and criticism. She writes, "Compassion honors our experience; it allows us to be intimate with the life of this moment as it is. Compassion makes our acceptance whole-hearted and complete."

We have the ability to change how we think and talk about ourselves. As with anything worthwhile, it takes practice. In psychotherapy, there is a technique called externalizing. Begin by identifying the critical inner voices that nag at you throughout the day. Then begin to see them not as internal messages, but as an external voice. Reframe the experience by saying in your mind or out loud: "This self-criticizing part of me is trying to convince me that I'm not good enough. I'm not interested in listening today." Making this shift can alter your relationship to those voices and make it easier to not give them power. Reinforce your awareness with an affirmative statement about what you want: "I am whole, perfect, and complete just as I am."

It takes intention and awareness to internally shift from disruptive emotions to self-affirming ones. We have a long history of stating the negative. It takes training to reframe the old messages we've been repeating to ourselves. When we observe our behavior and feelings, we can begin to manage them. Make it a practice to find optimistic, constructive, encouraging statements, such as: *I am enough. I am lovable and capable. I accept and honor myself.*

As we age, the importance of having good self-esteem cannot be overemphasized. Good self-esteem is the ability to accept ourselves, recognize our abilities, and value our worth, regardless of what others may think or say. It is an essential aspect of daily living that contributes positively to various areas of our lives, including our mental, emotional, and physical well-being.

Having good self-esteem promotes a sense of confidence and resilience, which become especially important as we age. It enables us to cope with life's challenges, setbacks, and changes in a more positive manner. With good self-esteem, we have a more positive outlook on life and are less likely to be overcome by stress, depression, or anxiety.

Years ago, I was visiting my dad, and I offered to change the batteries in the smoke detector. This was so painful for him because he knew he was no longer able to climb a ladder. For him it was a sign of weakness and failure. I listened with compassion. I shared how strong and supportive he had been his whole life and how appreciative I was. I was honored to be able to support him the way he supported me throughout my life. A short time later, I noticed some activities I could no longer do. I recalled what he said and could relate to how he was feeling.

When we live a life of intention, we move away from the self-defeating practice of comparing and competing. We are inspired to find role models whom we want to emulate. We connect with friends and associates who are encouraging and supportive. Instead of searching for our own acknowledgement, we recognize and celebrate the successes of those around us.

As we begin to peel away the layers of false beliefs and ideas about our bodies and ourselves, we touch on our awareness of the Divine, our connection with God. In *This Thing Called You*, Ernest Holmes states it perfectly: "There is a Divine awareness within you which will lead you upward and onward. Prepare yourself for the ascent, then fill your mental life with spiritual realization."

That still, small voice is our divine self. It wants to express. It wants to laugh, dance, run, skip, and celebrate. It is the presence of love that is whole, complete, and perfect.

As we release judgment of ourselves and those around us, we become aware of the exquisite beauty of nature around us. We begin to see ourselves as a temple for our living spirit and as a vessel to receive divine love.

Love is an inside job that begins with letting go of the pain from the past. Then there is an opening to express love. As we love ourselves, we begin to acknowledge and appreciate others. The more love we give, the more we receive. As we think about love, we become love.

It's time we acknowledge our beauty and accomplishments, accept our own compassion for being human, and celebrate our divinity. You would want that for your best friend, wouldn't you?

Prayer for Gracious Love

Today, I joyously step into the vitality
and energy of Spirit.
I recognize that Spirit is everywhere and in all things.
I see infinite potential in every person,
every event, and every idea.
I let go of any need to complain or judge
or separate myself from others, and I know that these
feelings no longer have power over my life.
I rejoice in the graciousness of Spirit,
knowing that I am blessed.
I enter this day with a grateful heart.

And so it is.

SPIRITUAL PRACTICE

Releasing Self-Judgment

(1) Recall your most recent experience with self-judgment.
- Record the experience in your journal.

Be sure to identify how the experience made you feel. Use the Conscious Journaling Technique at the end of Chapter One if you need help writing.

(2) What do you want instead?
- Describe what your life would be like if self-judgment and criticism were released from your thinking.

(3) Recite the following healing statement of truth any time you find yourself stuck in the experience of unworthiness:
- I release my belief in unworthiness.
  I accept the Presence of Love into my life.
  I am grateful I am free.

(4) Identify and record in your journal at least three things you are grateful for.

(5) Read the above Prayer for Gracious Love out loud at least once a day for seven days. Feel free to change the words to make it your own.

Download the chapter worksheet at
www.revchristine.com/books.

CHAPTER 3

Kick Doubt Out!

*Doubt is a pain too lonely
to know that faith is his twin brother.*

— KAHLIL GIBRAN

DOUBT IS A FABRICATION OF OUR IMAGINATION. As imagination fuels doubt, we begin to notice more and more limitation confronting us. As we imagine the effects of doubt, what we imagine becomes our reality—a truly vicious and nasty cycle.

> I asked a group of friends to read chapters of my book and critique them for me. I received this email from one of them and, needless to say, I was quite pleased.
>
> "I read the chapter, and all I can say is that I LOVE IT! I think it flows really well, has a great tone, good balance in terms of examples and quotes from other sources. I love it. It feels inspired. Keep up the awesome work!"
>
> What writer wouldn't want to get praise for their work? I felt great about her comments until about 4 a.m., the worry hour, when we wake up obsessing about what we did or didn't do and the

"what ifs" set in. That's when her email popped into my head again. What if she just said that to be nice? She's a pretty straightforward person. I don't think she would not have any feedback for me. What if she was afraid to tell me what she really thought? What if she's afraid to hurt my feelings, so she's holding back what she's really thinking? What if my writing is going nowhere? What if, what if, what if....

Sound familiar? This is the inner critic spreading doubt and fear in the middle of the night. Doubt is debilitating, disempowering, and diminishing. Doubt makes us afraid to take a step forward with the irrational fear of what could happen. What if I take the wrong step? What if things don't work out? *What if* is similar to the Energizer Bunny: It keeps going and going and going. It saps our energy and renders us ineffective.

Imagine what life would be like if doubt had stopped the inventor of the light bulb, the radio, or the gas-powered engine. How many times a day do we squash an idea because we don't know how to put it into action or fear what other people think? So often, I hear women say they wish they had more money. We don't realize that our ideas have the potential to bring us more money. And we have dozens of ideas each day, ideas that have the promise to make a difference in the world. Out of fear, we neglect them. We imagine that making the idea work would take too much effort, too much time, too much money. Potential brilliance or expression is then lost down the black hole of unfulfilled ideas.

AFFIRM:
I am grateful for my unlimited potential.

Jane Austen, known for her remarkable novels set in 19th century England, experienced significant trials before her talent was recognized. Austen's first novel, *Sense and Sensibility*, faced rejection from multiple publishers. Undeterred by these setbacks, she persevered and eventually found a publisher willing to print her work anonymously. Today, we celebrate her novels for their wit, social commentary, and timeless characters, and we celebrate Austen as one of the most renowned writers in English literature.

Jane Austen, Virginia Woolf, Sylvia Plath, and many other female writers learned to rise above rejection. Their courage serves as an inspiration, reminding us that determination and resilience are essential qualities in achieving our goals. Austen, Woolf, and Plath stand as powerful examples of women who refused to be silenced, leaving an enduring mark on the world of literature through their words, talent, and unwavering courage.

While it's hard enough to have the inner critic shouting at us in doubtful and negative voices, that critic has company. Very often we have well-meaning friends and family members around us who don't want to see us waste our time, money, and resources, who encourage us to find other outlets of expression. They tend to give advice and suggestions, often with the best of intentions, which can be more harmful than helpful.

AFFIRM:
I am grateful for the creative impulse that inspires me.

Oftentimes, rather than seeking professional guidance, women ask their friends, family, business associates, neighbors, and the salesclerk at the Nordstrom cosmetic counter for advice. It's a natural reaction to want to ask others for their opinion. The problem with this approach is that if you ask ten people, you will receive ten different answers. Instead of moving forward, this behavior often stirs up even more doubt. Instead of getting answers, we become confused.

There is a benefit to asking for support, as long as we are asking someone who has our best interest at heart. There is a commonly known saying: "It takes a village to raise a child." I suggest that it takes a village to support each human being. We are not meant to live in a vacuum. My spiritual mentor, writing coach, financial advisor, and prayer partner are just a few of the advisors in my village. I have developed meaningful relationships with each of them and know I can turn to any one of them to receive clear guidance and direction. As a result, I feel recharged and confident. The members of my village support me in getting in touch with my intuition. They are not in a hurry to give advice, but they ask me questions that get me to think.

I have observed that often we are more interested in sharing the drama of the story rather than we are in hearing the truth. Each time we repeat our tale of uncertainty and confusion, we expand our experience of doubt. We paint a picture of the unwanted experience, and now someone else sees it and connects us with the drama. Today's world of social media and reality TV have made conflict much more seductive than the possibility of peace and cooperation. Unfortunately, we are unaware that we lose precious time and energy as we share our doubts, confusion, and conflict. In fact, the process of repeating our self-doubt and criticism just expands our fears.

Fear

DOUBT STIRS FEELINGS of fear. Fear has powerful control over us, especially our fear of failure. It can be overwhelming because it often is associated with negative feelings, such as shame, embarrassment, and disappointment. The fear of failure can chip away at our self-esteem, causing us to question our abilities and worth. The fear of failure can keep us from stepping outside our comfort zone and pursuing our dreams and passions.

This lack of control over outcomes can cause feelings of helplessness and anxiety. The constant pressure to succeed in today's world and the emphasis on perfectionism can contribute to the fear of failure. Social media exposure and comparisons to others can amplify fears of not measuring up to what is seen as successful.

Even if we have ample experience and expertise, our fear of failure can keep us stuck. Consider Samantha, who was stymied by fear.

> Samantha's goal was to express her creativity through cooking. She found a great job with a progressive, growing company, where she was hired as the prep cook for a chef and assistant chef. She loved the people and the opportunity to be imaginative with her cooking. She was talented at coming up with original ways to prepare the entrées.
>
> The assistant chef left the company and the managers were in the process of hiring a new one. She was much more competent than the previous assistant, and I suggested that she apply for the job. Samantha, however, was quite adamant that she was not experienced enough and could not do the job.

Samantha's fear of failure overwhelmed her. In our work together, we looked at the fear and examined how the crippling belief in being a failure had shaped her life from childhood. Once Samantha recognized the source of the fear, she could reprogram her thinking. She applied for the assistant chef position, and the company eagerly hired her. Samantha would have stayed stuck if she had not been willing to look past her pain and into the possibilities.

Anything worth doing in life requires us to take appropriate risks. We step out into the unknown. We take a chance and declare our intentions to the world. Doubt and fear cause us to falter and stop. It can be disempowering when we continually question our actions and decisions.

> AFFIRM:
> I am willing to step out
> and take chances.

Similarly, fear of success is just as powerful as fear of failure. There is the mistaken notion that if we are successful, we will be changed in a negative way. It's true that we will change, but the fear of what the change will look like can be overwhelming. Success may bring new stresses and obstacles that we think we don't know how to face. Rather than embrace the changes that success may bring, we think it may just be easier to avoid progress altogether.

Avoidance

DO YOU EVER HAVE THOSE DAYS when doubt is so overwhelming that you want to get back under the comforter and spend the rest of the day there? Have you ever had a deadline to meet but spent the morning cleaning out the crumb tray of the toaster oven instead? Doubt triggers fear, fear sets off confusion, and confusion generates avoidance.

We have all had the experience of avoiding something we need to do. One of my career experiences was working as the assistant to the marketing manager for a software publisher. Sales had slowed down, and I knew the job was going nowhere, but the idea of job hunting and interviewing felt overwhelming. It was easier to avoid taking action. Eventually I was laid off. The universe sometimes offers a helping hand in times like this, giving us the push we need. By avoiding taking action myself, I created the experience of being powerless. I gave my power away, and someone else took action.

Have you ever noticed that someone else's problems are so much more interesting and manageable than your own? It is so easy to get involved and spend our precious time, energy, and advice on someone else's problems. When we dive in to solve the problems of our friends and neighbors, we set aside our own goals, desires, and dreams, and attempt to manage the lives of those around us instead. Being of service is profoundly rewarding. However, when we avoid taking care of our goals and dreams, we set the stage for future resentment and frustration.

AFFIRM:
I am empowered to take action.

Procrastination is another powerful form of avoidance. I'll do it tomorrow. Better yet, I'll do it next week when I have more time. Time thereby becomes our enemy. We convince ourselves that there are simply not enough hours in the day to do everything we want to do, and inertia sets in.

The biggest complaint I hear from my clients is their inability to move forward. They know what they are supposed to do. They just can't seem to do it. They become frustrated and often depressed because they simply are not doing the things in life that they know will bring them joy. Inertia is the immobilizing force that keeps us stuck and frustrated.

Some time ago, I worked with a client who was having trouble in her marriage. Here is her story of crippling inertia:

> Jessica had been married for twenty-three years. She lived through her husband's infidelities, verbal abusiveness, and controlling behavior. She just couldn't let go. The fear of living outside her marriage was greater than the sham of what her marriage had become. She suffered from depression, anxiety, and insomnia. She had suppressed her rage and frustration for too many years. Now the effects started to show up in her body. Unfortunately, rather than seek counseling or face the truth about their marriage, she and her husband went on an opulent European vacation, resulting in financial and emotional debt. Her marriage ended in a bitter divorce and bankruptcy.

It is difficult, if not nearly impossible, to stabilize on unstable territory. Eventually, we must face the fears and beliefs that hold us back. Until Jessica was ready to examine her fears and beliefs about her marriage and her life, she was held captive in her own life experience.

Doubt sparks hopeless thoughts and feelings of limitation: *I'm not smart enough, tall enough, educated enough, or talented enough to do the things I want to do. There is someone else who's better than me.*

Living in doubt, we often feel like we take three steps forward and two steps back. We may make some positive progress, but when doubt sneaks in, it can diminish our success. Often our limiting thoughts of doubt lead us into the trap of complaining.

Complaining

ACCUSATION, BLAME, AND CRITICISM: It's what I call the ABCs of complaining. It takes our attention off our own doubt and places it onto others. We often find ourselves complaining about the things we don't like or don't want in our lives. We convince ourselves that it's our friends and family members who cause the problems. If they would just get in, get out, or get going, we would be all right.

AFFIRM:
I consciously use words of faith and love.

If we believe our words have power, then our complaints keep our problems alive. Complaining reinforces the old pattern of thinking and keeps us stuck in the past. It takes concentration and practice to choose words of faith and love.

The law of attraction works both ways: Whatever you put your attention on increases. When we focus on what we want, we see more of what we want. When we put our attention on what isn't working, we continue to see more of the same. As we observe what is not working, our energy, enthusiasm, vitality, and passion begin to spiral downward, leaving us listless and lifeless.

Complaining, blaming, and criticizing are ways of life in today's world. We so often hear others complain about how miserable life is because of what someone said or didn't say. While it may provide temporary relief to vent our frustrations, it ultimately does little to change the situation.

Emma Curtis Hopkins tells us, "Don't complain. You will feel less spiritual inspiration when you are mourning, whining, and complaining, but when you praise and describe the Good, you will feel full of spiritual fervor."

To break free from this cycle, we must consciously choose our words with intention. We must practice speaking in terms of faith and love, even when it feels difficult or uncomfortable. It may take time and effort, but the results are worth it.

What do I want instead? This is an important question that takes us out of the downward spiral and lifts us into the realm of possibility. Possibilities stimulate our imagination, causing us to look upward and beyond the current experience. Opening to imagination opens us to the limitless expression of Spirit.

Imagination...is more important than knowledge. Knowledge is limited. Imagination encircles the world.

— ALBERT EINSTEIN

Spiritual Principle:
Where my imagination leads, my reality will follow.

THERE IS A PART OF THE BRAIN called the reticular activating system. It works like a filter between your conscious mind and subconscious mind. When we think about something we want, we start to notice it everywhere. If you think about a red Lexus ES, suddenly you will see red Lexus ES cars wherever you go. Also, the reticular activating system of the brain does not know the difference between what is imagined and what is real. The effect of our doubtful imagination stirs our emotions, pumps up the adrenaline, and gets the heart racing, at which point we are in full-fledged stress mode.

Try this exercise: Imagine right now that there is a big bowl of beautiful just-picked-from-the-tree lemons in front of you, and next to it is a small paring knife. Imagine picking up a lemon and sniffing it. Notice the fragrance and the smoothness of the skin. Now pick up the paring knife, and cut into the lemon. Cut a small slice and bring it up to your nose and take a sniff. Notice anything happening in your body? The salivating glands begin to work overtime. Even though the lemon is invisible, the brain doesn't know that. Our imagination is so powerful that it can cause a physical reaction in the body.

As humans, we often find ourselves worrying about what we don't want in life: failure, rejection, loss, and pain. These fears can consume our minds, making us feel powerless and stuck in an endless cycle of negativity. But what if we shifted our focus from the fear of what we don't want to the power of imagining what we do want?

Spending time visualizing our dreams and desires can be a transformative experience, giving us the motivation and inspiration to take action toward achieving them. When we imagine what we want, we tap into our creativity, intuition, and deeper sense of purpose. We can see ourselves living the life we truly desire, feeling the emotions of joy, love, excitement, and fulfillment that come with it. The power of our thoughts and imagination is truly immense. As we channel our energy into thoughts of what we want, we attract more of it into our lives. Our actions become aligned with our intentions, and we begin to see opportunities and possibilities we may not have noticed before.

Set the intention to focus on the power of your imagination and dream big. The more we focus on what we want, the more we manifest it in our reality.

Imagining the possibilities of a life of harmony, peace, and prosperity changes our energy, down to the very cells of our bodies. Each one of us has the power to transform doubt into faith.

Speaking with purpose is an essential part of our spiritual practice and is so easily ignored. It can be so easy to complain, blame, and focus on the things we don't like. It takes discipline and persistence to speak with good intention. Resist the need to complain.

Rev. Will Bowen, author of *A Complaint Free World*, challenged members of his congregation to go twenty-one days without complaining. He gave them each a wrist band and suggested that every time they complained, they move the wristband from one wrist to the other. His idea motivated people around the world. More than eight million bracelets have been sent to people in more than 100 countries.

Women are great doers. We can handle all the things thrown at us for ourselves and our families. We are trained to multi-task, multi-process, multi-schedule, and leap over tall buildings in a single bound. We are so adept at doing that we forget to ask for help. We believe it's risky to delegate to someone else because they just can't do the job as well as we can. It is just so difficult to let go of control.

AFFIRM:
I am willing to ask for help.

As we develop our faith, we expand our awareness, and we realize that we do not have to walk the path alone. Operating from the ego or human personality, we can fall into doubt because we think we need to figure out what we are going to do next. A necessary step in our spiritual growth is to practice placing our faith and trust in the universal good. Marianne Williamson reminds us, "Faith is believing that the universe is on our side, and the universe knows what it is doing."

There have been many times over the years on my spiritual journey that I stood seemingly at the edge of the void, not knowing what step to take next. I had nowhere to turn but within. As I placed my trust in God, not in the world, the next step was revealed.

> I had found what I believed to be my perfect job. It was as if the job description were written for me. After three very positive interviews, I was sure the job was mine. I visualized myself driving to the office building every morning and working with the great people I met in the interview process. I could see myself as a team member with their staff and supporting their clients. The call finally came from Michael, one of the owners of the company. The news was not good. Sixty-three people applied for the position. The owners

narrowed it down to two applicants, and I was one of them. But they gave the job to my competitor. In my stunned state of mind, I somehow found the words and thanked Michael for the opportunity, asked him to keep me in mind for the future and hung up the phone.

I was devastated. I was so confused. I so clearly saw myself in the position and now it was gone. I called my spiritual mentor. She reminded me that if it wasn't this job, there was something better waiting in the wings. I took a walk around the block and centered myself. Instead of fixating on what I didn't have, I used the opportunity to look forward to the possibilities. I immediately picked up the phone and called some other companies where I had applied for positions.

Within the hour, I received a call back from Michael. He said the applicant they offered the job to turned them down because the benefits didn't meet her needs. He was surprised by her response and apologetically inquired if I was still interested in the job. I graciously accepted the offer.

Faith is an individual process of growth, patience, and willingness. It is up to us to continue to let go of the pictures of doubt and replace them with how we intend to express love in the world. Ultimately, love is our highest vision. Whatever we desire in our hearts, whether it is something we want to accomplish in the world or something greater we envision for our families, it is always about expressing love.

AFFIRM:

I express love in my thoughts, words, and actions.

Faith is the freedom in knowing that whatever I need will be provided, whether it's having the strength to face the day, the courage to speak my truth, or the desire to help a loved one. Faith is appreciating each day as a treasure and every experience as a gift. Ernest Holmes teaches us in *The Science of Mind:* "If we will have faith in ourselves, faith in each other, in the Universe and in God, that faith will light the place in which we find ourselves, and by that light we will be able to see that all is Good."

Let's kick doubt out. There is no longer room for doubt in your consciousness. There is no longer room for doubt in your experience of life. You have the faith to live life fully and with joy.

Prayer of Faith

I recognize at the center of all life
is an Infinite Power guiding and directing
me in all my activities.
I surrender any belief in doubt and any experience
or belief that I am not enough.
I release any feelings of fear and any
tendency to avoid and complain.
I speak with good purpose and think loving
thoughts of those around me.
I walk with intention, knowing I am guided
and directed along my spiritual journey.
I am truly grateful for the newness of this day
and the many blessings I receive.

And so it is.

SPIRITUAL PRACTICE

Releasing Doubt

(1) Recall your most recent encounter with doubt.
   - Record the experience in your journal.

   Be sure to identify how the experience made you feel. Use the Conscious Journaling Technique at the end of Chapter One if you need help writing.

(2) What do you want instead?
   - Describe what your life would be like if doubt was released from your thinking.

(3) Recite the following healing statement of truth any time you find yourself stuck in the experience of unworthiness:
   - I release my belief in doubt. I accept a deepening of faith into my life. I am grateful I am free.

(4) Identify and record in your journal at least three things you are grateful for.

(5) Read the above Prayer of Faith out loud at least once a day for seven days. Feel free to change the words to make it your own.

Download the chapter worksheet at
www.revchristine.com/books.

CHAPTER 4

Leave Your
Victim Self Behind

*You might say, "What a dreadful day,"
without realizing that the cold, the wind, and the rain or
whatever conditions you react to are not dreadful.
They are as they are. What is dreadful is your reaction,
your inner resistance to it, and the emotion
that is created by that resistance.*

— EKHART TOLLE

THINKING LIKE A VICTIM, or "victim thinking," keeps us anchored in the past and prevents us from moving forward. It occurs when we hold onto the experience of being wronged and believe we are powerless to change our circumstances. This type of thinking can be especially toxic because it breeds an attitude of helplessness and self-pity that can make it difficult to take action.

Take a quick inventory. Notice when your thoughts lean toward blaming others for your pain and avoiding taking responsibility. It might show up in phrases such as: *I can't help it, that's just the way I am. It's not my fault. Those people just don't like me. I never seem to get ahead.*

When we engage in victim thinking, we fixate on the past and the ways we have been harmed. We may replay an incident over and over again in our minds, ruminating on the what-ifs and feeling a deep sense of anger, hurt, or shame. While it's natural to experience these emotions in the aftermath of a traumatic event, it's important to acknowledge that holding onto them for too long can be detrimental to our mental health and well-being.

One of the negative consequences of victim thinking is that it can affect our relationships with others. When we view ourselves as powerless victims, we may be more likely to blame others for our problems or lash out at those who try to help us. This attitude can create a self-fulfilling prophecy, in which we push away the people who care about us and isolate ourselves from the support we need.

To move beyond victim thinking, we must learn to let go of the past and focus on taking action in the present. This means accepting responsibility for our part in the situation and looking for ways we can make positive changes.

Ultimately, victim thinking is a mindset that keeps us stuck in the past and prevents us from living our lives to the fullest. By letting go of our victimhood and embracing our own experience, we can overcome the challenges we face and create a brighter future for ourselves.

It is so easy to take personally what others say to us. In reality, if we feel insulted or offended by someone, it most likely has nothing to do with us. They are reacting in their own mind to their own conditioning and thinking. It can be difficult to remember that when we feel offended. Often the resulting pain can be so intense we store it away, only to see it erupt at a later time and place.

AFFIRM:
I am willing to take responsibility
for my experiences.

When we are unaware of our victim mentality, we suffer. It feels as if everyone is against us and that our goals and dreams don't really count. Our self-esteem takes a hit, and no amount of success can stay with us for long in this state of being.

No doubt about it, life can be challenging. Most people experience some sort of hardship and adversity. However, when we hang onto those experiences and use them as the guiding viewpoints of life, we live as victims.

We have great role models who experienced adversity but refused to identify themselves as victims. Helen Keller was blind and deaf, yet as a young child, she learned to read French, German, Greek, and Latin in braille. Elizabeth Blackwell faced criticism and ridicule and was rejected by twenty-nine medical colleges, but it never stopped her from pursuing her dream of becoming the first female doctor. Rosa Parks stood up against racism and changed the world by keeping her seat on the bus. All three of these champions shared a common trait. By accepting personal responsibility, facing fears, and taking action, these women moved out of the victim role and into freedom.

When in the victim role, we look to others to make things happen. Unfortunately, it doesn't occur to us that we can create our own happiness. Simply waiting for circumstances to change renders us powerless.

Powerlessness

WHEN WE FEEL POWERLESS, we often believe we need someone else to come along and save us. Think about the fairy tales we were told as children about beautiful women who were powerless and needed to be rescued. Snow White was fed a poison apple, Sleeping Beauty fell into a deep sleep after receiving a curse from a wicked witch, and Cinderella suffered abuse by her angry stepmother. All of them were helpless victims. Suddenly, a prince—always handsome, strong, patient, and kind—appeared to make life perfect again. Naturally, he carried the beautiful woman (now a princess) off into the sunset to begin a new and perfect life together.

I often ask women taking my relationship workshops how many are still waiting for their princes to show up. Usually, half the group raises their hands. There is a persisting belief among women that somehow life will be better when we find a man to take care of us. The fantasy is that a man will rush in, take over the chores, discipline the kids, fix the car, solve our money problems, cherish and worship us, and we will live happily ever after. The truth is, if we don't face our beliefs in feeling powerless and helpless, a new man will bring old problems in a big way.

AFFIRM:
I am empowered to take action in my life.

What's the payoff? There is a comfort in living in the place of powerlessness. Not much is expected of us.

Living in a state of powerlessness can be alluring. We feel a sense of relief, as though we are absolved of responsibility when we are unable to affect change in our surroundings. It seems like an easier option, to simply give up and relinquish control.

However, this surrendering of power can often result in a negative spiral of hopelessness. And it can be disempowering, as we give away our power to others. We often unintentionally give away our rights, our voices, and our decision-making abilities. The dawn of the Me Too Movement brought to light sexual abuse, domestic violence, and harassment. The movement has been transformational in engaging community-based activism and activating national legislation and global policy to protect women. Giving up our power is not to be taken lightly.

When we believe we can't control the circumstances around us, we often feel dismayed. Very often, that dismay enables denial.

Denial

DENIAL IS A CONDITION in which we spend much of our time arranging and rearranging our outward conditions, while ignoring the fears and limitations we feel inside. It sometimes can be related to the phrase "rearranging the deck chairs on the Titanic." The ship is sinking, but we are in denial that there is anything to change.

Denial can be a surreal state of mind where we struggle to face the truths and realities that we fear or find too difficult to accept. This state of mind keeps us oblivious to the fact that these fears and limitations are still present within us, regardless of how we dress up our lives externally. It is a way of deceiving ourselves into believing that everything is fine when it is not. Denial allows us to block out unpleasant thoughts, feelings, and perceptions that challenge our comfort zone, thereby making us avoid dealing with our conflicts. The danger of denial lies in its potential to make us feel trapped in our own personal illusions, leaving us vulnerable and unable to face the challenges life throws our way. It prevents us from experiencing emotional growth, keeps us stagnant, and can stunt our personal development.

To break free from denial, we must be willing to confront our fears and limitations, even if it means facing discomfort or pain. We must open up to the possibility that our perceptions of reality may not be entirely accurate, and we need to challenge our limiting beliefs to create positive change in our lives. It takes courage and self-awareness to overcome denial, but it is only by facing our fears and limitations that we can grow and create happy and fulfilling lives.

Denial can come in many forms. For example, neglecting to balance the checkbook and then wondering why money vanished before the end of the month is denial in action. Denial is a relationship gone bad and refusing to let it go. Denial is getting stuck in the victim mentality and thinking that everyone is just luckier than we are.

My own experience with denial exposed how I was more interested in looking good than having an honest relationship.

I met someone through a dating service. We connected and sparks flew. On our next date, he came over and cooked dinner for me. (Now I was hooked). He was a busy attorney and not as available as I wanted. I thought it unusual that we never went to his house, but I didn't want to rock the boat of this new exciting relationship. I invited him as my guest to a friend's wedding that was coming up in three weeks. I couldn't wait to show him off to my friends.

I noticed he became aloof and distant over the next two weeks. Taking him to the wedding became so important to me—more important than our relationship (or lack of one). I called several times to make sure he was still going to attend. Finally, the big day arrived. The wedding was on a boat that slowly cruised down the river, confining us for several hours. The afternoon was a nightmare for me. He ignored me when I talked to him. He refused to sit with me at dinner and left me alone while he drank at the bar. I put on a happy face and visited with my friends the best I could. Finally, the boat docked, and he deposited me at my doorstep never to be seen again.

I was devastated. I cried for days, feeling rejected, hopeless, and unworthy.

If I had felt confident about who I was and had not been knee-deep in unworthiness and powerlessness about my life, I would have called him and canceled our date for the wedding when I noticed his detachment. Instead, I was more interested in bringing a date than truly developing a loving relationship. My neediness kept me clinging to him instead of letting him go. I paid for my denial in the end. In truth, all I was doing was avoiding my emotions.

These are two ways we can avoid feeling our emotions: distracting ourselves by masking the emotion or appeasing others so we don't rock the boat. Neither addresses the pain we are in. Both simply suppress it. All too often, the underlying belief is that we are simply not good enough.

AFFIRM:
I believe in myself.

Too often, we are held hostage in the tower of our thinking, feeling imprisoned, isolated, and alone. We paint a picture in our minds of people ignoring and rejecting us. We rarely question the false beliefs we hold about ourselves, and as a result, we see the outcome of these beliefs all around us. The first time someone slights us or ignores us convinces that we are right: *The world is a cruel place. See, I told you so.* All too often this perceived confirmation leads to or reinforces a false belief about our unworthiness.

Unworthiness

A HARSH WORD, A DISAPPROVING LOOK, or a harmless comment can catapult us into feelings of unworthiness. Whatever sense of self-worth we have can be diminished in an instant because of another's actions. The moment we transfer power over to another, we feel both helpless and hopeless.

AFFIRM:
I am lovable.

The need to be loved and accepted by others makes us vulnerable to feeling hurt, criticized, and judged. We tend to embrace judgments and criticisms as the reflections of our unworthiness. It is difficult to see beyond our pain and suffering and imagine the possibility of moving forward.

> Naomi had been abused by her father when she was seven years old. The condition of being a victim followed her throughout her life. Now 35 years old, she was divorced and desperate to find a relationship that was supportive and not abusive. Her current relationship was exceptionally painful because her partner was verbally abusive and demeaning toward her. All she wanted was to be loved.
>
> Naomi also was setting a painful example for her daughter. Her seven-year-old daughter daily watched her mother's pain. She observed her mother trying so hard to be loved, wandering from one unhealthy relationship to another, and giving up her self-esteem and self-worth in the process.

When self-esteem is depleted, we often allow ourselves to be bullied. As women, we have been culturally conditioned to be nice and to be passive, which can often result in allowing others to bully or manipulate us into making decisions from a place of stress rather than choice. The pattern of unworthiness can be so all-encompassing that we don't know anything else is possible.

We may feel like we don't deserve to be treated with respect and kindness, so we settle for less than we deserve. This can manifest in many areas of our lives, from our relationships and jobs to our personal goals and aspirations. When we allow ourselves to be bullied, we give away our power. We become passive observers in our own lives, waiting for someone else to make decisions for us. This can be incredibly damaging to our self-esteem and sense of worth. It's important to recognize that bullying and manipulation are not acceptable behaviors from anyone, no matter the circumstances. By setting boundaries and speaking up for ourselves, we can begin to take back our power and reclaim control of our lives.

It is crucial to work on improving our self-esteem and learning to value ourselves. This can involve seeking help from a therapist or counselor, practicing self-care, and surrounding ourselves with supportive and uplifting people.

It may take time and effort to break free from the cycle of unworthiness and bullying, but it's vital for our personal growth and happiness. We deserve to be treated with respect and kindness, and it's up to us to demand that from others and ourselves.

When we don't stand up for ourselves, we both model and pass on the experience of victimhood to the next generation, making it even more challenging for them to break the cycle.

AFFIRM:
I am confident and speak with
clarity and purpose.

There are times in abusive situations when the victims reach the end of their rope and then become the aggressors. They can begin to lash out at others, so they can finally take dominion over something in their life. Anger and frustration from the pain reaches its limits, and the need to punish takes over. The next person they see will most likely be on the receiving end of victimization.

How does this lashing out show up for us as women? One way is gossip. We gossip about others to make ourselves feel superior. I have observed that often, women will leave others out of their social circle as way to exert power or strength. In that moment, we become the bullies instead of feeling bullied. However, whatever superiority we feel is fleeting. The false sense of power is like kryptonite that saps our strength and depletes our energy. The thrill of false power soon wears off and the cycle starts over again.

Right now, stand up and shake off those old beliefs. There is a way out.

Spiritual Principle:
What I take responsibility for, I can change.

IF I BLAME AND ACCUSE others, I feel helpless to change the circumstances around me. I've given away my power and my ability to take action.

Chapter 4 — Leave Your Victim Self Behind

It is essential to recognize that there is comfort in powerlessness, but, in the long run, it does not lead to growth or success. By adopting a proactive approach to life, we can change our situations and alter our trajectories for the better. We must be willing to take the responsibility for our lives and understand that we are in control of our destinies.

Gracing yourself with responsibility for everything that happens in your life leaves your spirit whole, and leaves you free to choose again.

— BEN & ROZAMUND ZANDER

By accepting responsibility, we empower ourselves to influence our circumstances. We become active participants in our lives, taking steps toward progress and success. It is only when we begin to let go of the comfort of helplessness that we gain the power to create change.

If I take responsibility for my condition or circumstances, then I can begin to change what I believe and think and eventually how I behave. Responsibility is not about blaming ourselves. Responsibility is the ability to respond, the freedom to take action. It is the power to change. When we take responsibility, we face our fears and take steps to move past them.

AFFIRM:
I am willing to take responsibility
for my actions.

By identifying our victim-thoughts and becoming conscious of them, we move ourselves out of being reactive and into making choices about how to take steps to move forward. Are you feeling slighted by a friend? Give them a call. Worried about a project at work? Ask for help from an associate. By taking action, we move from being powerless to feeling empowered.

By devoting ourselves to the spiritual practices of meditation, journaling, and prayer, we turn away from the conditions of the world. Spiritual practice opens us to the divine nature of God, which is always available to us. If you are feeling separate from God, who moved? We are the ones blocking the flow. We are the ones who have the ability to release our victim self and move into the center of wholeness.

The pathway to freedom can show up in quiet ways. In fact, I found that even in my dream state, I could take charge of my life. Over the years, I've had a recurring dream where I lose my purse. Sometimes I was in a store, sometimes walking down the street. Suddenly, I would notice that my purse was missing. I would panic and become afraid. I knew I was working through my belief of feeling like a victim, as though someone took my good from me. One night while I was still dreaming, I became aware in my dream state. I recognized this was the same recurring dream and that I had the power to change the scenario. In that moment, I moved from being the victim to becoming the victor in the dream. I took charge and retrieved my purse and vanquished powerlessness in my dream, paving the way for me to do the same in waking life.

Chapter 4 — Leave Your Victim Self Behind

*As you begin to think more about how you can
love your way through life, rather than about how you
have to battle your way through life,
love will reveal to you its secret success powers.*

— CATHERINE PONDER

Another way to become free from being a victim is to forgive. When we don't forgive, we stay in the struggle. It is a burden we carry in our souls, one that keeps us prisoners to the past. We are in bondage with anger, bitterness, and resentment. When we don't forgive, we make it difficult to move forward in life because there is a wall that separates us from love. Mother Theresa reminds us, "If we really want to love, we must learn how to forgive."

Forgiveness does not mean we condone the pain or suffering that may have occurred. It is an opportunity to let go. It takes a great deal of courage to let go. When we do, it is one of the most important processes that will bring harmony to life and peace to our soul. We are free to express love into the world.

AFFIRM:
I choose love instead of fear.

When we choose love instead of fear, we change the nature and the quality of our relationships. Love is expansive, while fear contracts. We cannot experience both fear and love at the same time. Choosing love brings greater joy, freedom, and peace. Buddha said this so eloquently:

"When we conquer by force, our enemy remains angry. When we conquer with love, there is no after-sorrow."

Once we have awareness of our victim self and demonstrate the desire to change our circumstances, we can see the results. Being willing to be the observer of our behavior is the first step in living a more fulfilling spiritual life. When we take the time to look beyond the appearances of the world, we can take steps toward living more consciously and more compassionately. The word compassion comes after compass in the dictionary. Perhaps compassion is the compass to show us how to love.

By consciously identifying victim thoughts and reframing them, we can begin to lift ourselves out of our victimhood and into the presence of faith. Wayne Dyer shares: "With everything that has happened to you, you can either feel sorry for yourself or treat what has happened as a gift. Everything is either an opportunity to grow or an obstacle to keep you from growing. You get to choose."

The power we ultimately search for cannot be found in the physical world. As we deepen in faith we are empowered and allow Spirit to work through us. There is less attention on our ego getting results and more appreciation for the Divine expressing through us. The light of God within is the power we seek, and God's power is love.

Love has the power to heal, to forgive, and to make new. Turning to our divine self instead of our victim self, we are powerful, experience our worthiness, and live in harmony and freedom.

Prayer for Receiving Grace

My heart and mind are open
to accept the divine presence of love that is God.
I know love moves into the very cells of my being,
bringing light, harmony, and peace.
I accept guidance to willingly let go of any belief in
victim thinking and any experience of feeling
powerless, unworthiness, or denial.
I invite the healing presence of love to wash away
any distrust or disbelief.
I know I am guided in all that I do.
I walk in Infinite Power, which is grace, and I welcome
and embrace grace into my life this day.
I enter this day with a grateful heart and receive the
blessings love has in store for me.

And so it is.

SPIRITUAL PRACTICE

Releasing Victim-Thinking

(1) Recall your most recent encounter with victim-thinking.
   - Record the experience in your journal.

   Be sure to identify how the experience made you feel. Use the Conscious Journaling Technique at the end of Chapter One if you need help writing.

(2) Who do you need to forgive?
   - Write a letter in your journal to someone you need to forgive.

   Share your emotions, fears, and reactions. DO NOT SEND IT. This practice enables you to release old emotions. Write as many letters as you need, until you feel free.

(3) Recite the following healing statement of truth anytime you find yourself stuck in the experience of unworthiness.
   - I release my belief that I am a victim.
     I am empowered with Divine Grace.
     I am grateful I am free.

(4) Identify and record in your journal at least three things you are grateful for.

(5) Read the above Prayer for Receiving Grace out loud at least once a day for seven days. Feel free to change the words to make it your own.

Download the chapter worksheet at
www.revchristine.com/books.

CHAPTER 5

This, Too, Shall Pass

You do not have a problem except the one that is in your own mind, and you put it there!

— MYRTLE FILLMORE

HUMAN NATURE IS FAR FROM PERFECT, and so is the world we live in. Pain and suffering are inevitable. During our lifetime, we will experience physical pain from injury and sickness. We will also experience emotional pain, such as frustration, sadness, disappointment, rejection, and depression. While physical ailments often are unpredictable and unavoidable, we can control the feelings we have about them.

> As I was writing this chapter, I came down with a head cold. Coughing, sneezing, and a headache sent me back to bed. I was so frustrated. I thought about all the things I had to do that were not getting done and worried about the appointments I might have to cancel later in the week. I was frustrated about not being able to exercise and how easily I was tired from any activity. I stressed about my upcoming workshop and the plane trip next month. STOP! I realized I was suf-

fering not only from the symptoms of my cold but also from the emotional turmoil that was created in my mind. The cold symptoms were mild and manageable. The emotional turmoil was excruciating. As long as I was thinking about the future, I was suffering.

As I was feeling sorry for myself, I thought about what friends and acquaintances have shared about their personal anguish: feeling rejected by their children, feeling ignored by business associates, being passed over for promotion, feeling alone, feeling sad over the physical pain and loss of mobility from an injury, and self-loathing for not completing a project ... the list goes on and on.

Regardless of the best laid plans, life often will give us challenges and obstacles along the way. We suffer when our minds are stuck in a pattern of negative belief, and our emotions run wild because of it.

Whatever the reason, suffering causes us to fall into victim consciousness, feeling powerless and helpless. When we are in pain, we tend to blame others, to feel guilty, to worry, and to tumble into the pitfalls of suffering.

Blame

IN TODAY'S WORLD, playing the blame game is quite popular. We have drifted into the habit of finding a scapegoat, someone to blame for the enormous problems we face. We blame the government, stock market, banks, wealthy people, poor people, big business, other countries, our parents, and the internet. It's become so common that many of us don't even realize how often we do it. We often feel the need to assign blame so we can validate our own opinions and beliefs.

But the truth is, the blame game is a dangerous one. It only serves to create division and animosity, rather than bringing us closer together to solutions. When we blame others, we remove ourselves from the responsibility of finding solutions. We become passive observers, waiting for someone else to fix the problem.

Instead of blaming others, we need to take a hard look at ourselves. What can we do to make things better? How can we contribute to positive change? When we stop looking for someone to blame and focus instead on taking action steps, we can create a better world for everyone.

AFFIRM:
My heart is open, and I speak with loving words.

We tend to blame others to help relieve the pain of suffering. We blame others to avoid taking responsibility for ourselves.

> Deanna complained about her business associate, Bob, and how irresponsible he was. She would send him qualified referrals and he would not follow up with the potential clients. Bob alienated other business partners as well with his erratic behavior. Deanna began each session with me by blaming Bob for the difficulties in her life and how she wished she could send him away. As long as Deanna blamed Bob, she neglected her own goals.

I suggested that Deanna move her attention away from what Bob was doing and instead focus on her clients. I asked her to think about what she wanted instead of what she didn't want. Eventually she was able to have compassion for Bob and his own struggle to build his business. She changed her focus, took attention off what he was doing, and found she could be in peace with him. Bob left his position soon after and found another field of employment.

As long as Deanna kept her attention on Bob, she was powerless. She allowed her energy to be drained by his actions. Once she recognized her behavior, she was able to have compassion for his struggles. She quit blaming him and put her attention on her business. She found another business associate who was a better match for her. She found more peace in her personal and business life.

Deanna used Bob as an avoidance mechanism to ignore her own problems. He only appeared to be the source of her challenges. In reality, the only power he had was what she gave him.

We often blame our parents for their past actions, believing that their actions are the cause of our pain. If we could only realize that parents are people, too. They, too, struggled with their own limiting beliefs and did the best they could. When we view our parents with compassion, we can let go of our blame and accusations and be set free.

AFFIRM:
I accept and appreciate those around me and release any need to blame.

As long as we blame others, we do not take responsibility for ourselves. We have the capacity to take control of our situations and guide the direction of our lives. There are certain factors that are out of our control, such as political, social, and economic conditions. As we continue to build awareness and consciousness, we recognize that we have the ability to respond rather than react to those situations and adjust our behaviors and lifestyles.

When we are stuck in the blame game, we don't limit the blame to others. We also blame ourselves. When we blame ourselves for experiences in which we have no control, we drain our energy and enthusiasm. And eventually, we begin to feel guilty.

Guilt

GUILT IS THE FEELING OF responsibility for some offense, crime or wrongdoing, whether real or imagined. One way of seeing guilt is as a safety valve for human behavior. There are standards for doing the right thing. That nagging voice that raises guilt causes us to pause and observe our personal actions.

Guilt helps us recognize and correct our mistakes. It reminds us to act in accordance with our values and beliefs. It is a natural emotion that signals to us that we have violated a moral code or ethical standard. When we feel guilty, we become aware of the consequences of our actions and seek to make amends.

Guilt also becomes problematic when it is excessive or irrational. When we feel guilty for things that are beyond our control or for events that have no bearing on our lives, we can find ourselves led to feelings of hopelessness, anxiety, and depression. It is important to recognize when our guilt is unwarranted and to seek help if these feelings become overwhelming.

Ultimately, guilt can serve as a powerful motivator for positive change. By acknowledging our mistakes, taking responsibility for our actions, and making amends when necessary, we can learn from our past behaviors and become more aware in the future. Instead of avoiding guilt, we can see it as an opportunity for growth and self-improvement.

The challenge for us as women is that we also can feel guilty for something we did not do. We feel guilty when we believe we have let someone down or did not do something to the best of our ability. We feel guilty because we often imagine that others are in pain and suffering because of our actions. Do we gain anything by feeling guilty? Is there any benefit to it? The payoff is that we stay stuck in the same behavior.

AFFIRM:
I now choose to recognize the magnificence of my being.

The fact is that we can get into the trap of using guilt to avoid action instead of taking responsibility. Guilt causes a downward spiral that makes it is difficult to decide what to do next. We stay trapped in our feelings instead of moving forward to take action to correct it.

Jessica shared with me her intense guilt about her family. Her sister cares for her elderly parents, and Jessica suffers with guilt-ridden feelings around not being there to help. Rather than wallowing in guilt, I suggested she talk with her sister on a regular basis to get an update on her parents' health. I reminded her that she already made regular visits to her home town to be there to help out. Jessica offered to help pay for a personal aide to run errands and take her parents to the doctor. Instead of staying stuck in guilt, she was able to find ways to help share the responsibility and ease her sister's burden.

Guilt can be a detractor that keeps us stuck or a motivator that helps us find both solutions and answers. We can feel guilty about not exercising, or we can go for a ten-minute walk. We can feel guilty about not visiting a friend in the hospital, or we can call them with warm wishes. We can feel guilty about not finishing a project, or we can set a new goal to get back on track.

Every day is a new opportunity to start fresh. The next time guilt takes over your thoughts and emotions, set a plan of action. Make a decision. Move forward on a goal. Or, of course, you always have the choice to worry instead.

Worry

I AM A TRAINED WORRIER—and I was trained by the best. A powerful childhood memory I have is of my mother waiting for my dad to come home after work.

Chapter 5 — This, Too, Shall Pass

It was a snowy winter day in upstate New York. My dad had a 45-minute commute each way from his job. My mother would pace from the kitchen, where she was preparing dinner, to the living room window looking out into the street. She would peer out the window and then walk back to the kitchen. Not once or twice, but many times. It finally occurred to me that it would be helpful if I joined her. Finally my dad arrived home, safe and sound. From watching my mom's actions, I came to believe that worry was the assurance that my dad would come home safely.

From my mother's excellent training in the art of worry, I spent many years worried about everything: homework projects, Girl Scout cookie sales, passing grades, winter storms, job interviews, health challenges, relationships—the list is endless. My problems were nothing compared to world issues: war, women's equality, rising gas prices, political elections, and the desperate need for world peace.

AFFIRM:
All that I need is already provided for.

I learned that worrying does not prevent anything from happening, nor does it save anyone from suffering. I learned that I really gain no control by worrying. It is a deeply embedded learned behavior, and I am still working on releasing the habit.

Worrying is a natural response to fear and uncertainty, but I've come to realize that it's not really a productive one. No matter how much I worry, it won't change the outcome of a situation or prevent something from happening. In fact, all it really does is add unnecessary stress and anxiety to my life.

Worrying doesn't actually give us any control over a situation. If anything, it takes away the control we have by clouding our judgment and decision-making abilities. It's like trying to drive a car with your eyes closed: You might feel like you're doing something to steer the car, but in reality, you're just putting yourself in danger.

Of course, breaking the habit of worrying is easier said than done. It is a learned behavior developed over many years, so it's not something that will disappear overnight. Personally, I pay attention when I start to worry and consciously choose to let go of anxious thoughts. I also remind myself that worrying won't change the outcome of a situation, so I focus on what I can control and let the rest play out as it will.

Overall, I learned that worrying isn't worth the emotional energy it requires. Instead of spending my time and energy on worrying, I practice cultivating a sense of calm and trust in myself and the universe. I know that the more I practice, the easier it will become. When I find myself worrying, I pull out this affirmation from Catherine Ponder: "Divine Love is doing is perfect work here and now. Divine Love harmonizes, Divine Love adjusts, Divine Love prospers. Divine Love foresees everything and richly provides every good thing for my life now. Divine Love is now victorious."

Worry is projection. When we project what we think will happen, we worry about an event that has not occurred. It is fantasy, not reality. Worry does not add anything to life, it just detracts. In fact, it increases the stress and strain. Whatever we are worried about shows up multiplied.

Spiritual Principle:
Whatever I put my attention on increases.

IF WE THINK ABOUT LACK, we see more lack. If we think about bad things happening, we are more aware of all the negative things in the world. If we think about something we are grateful for, we are more aware of positive outcomes.

AFFIRM:
I live with an attitude of gratitude.

Dr Emmett Fox, author, teacher, and healer, developed the concept of "The Golden Key." He taught that the key to peace of mind is to take attention away from the current problem and put it on God instead. In other words, stop worrying about the problem and put your thoughts on God or the highest idea of Good in your life. When you do this, you will be amazed at how your mind clears and things begin working out more easily. In fact, I have noticed they usually work out better than I even thought possible.

This is not a suggestion that you bury your head in the sand and ignore all the events going on in the world around us. The Golden Key suggests that we acknowledge the issues of the day and focus on the highest thought we can. This simple technique can stop the downward spiral and help us feel empowered instead of powerless.

Use your energy to take positive steps in your life. Take action toward building your business, finishing a project, learning a new skill, or expanding your client base. Worried about money? Talk with a financial expert about your goals. Feel helpless? Reach out a helping hand to someone around you. You will be amazed at how energized you will feel.

There are times when we just cannot change the circumstances. We may not like our situation, but we accept it and deal with it the best we can.

> A powerful example of this attitude comes from Boston Marathon bombing survivors, Jessica Kensky and Patrick Downes. They were newlyweds in 2013, looking forward to building their new life together. Both of them were at the finish line when the two bombs went off. Each of them lost a leg. Because of complications, two years later Jessica lost her other leg. Their recovery was extremely challenging. Their parents cared for them, and they said they felt like children again. As they regained their strength and abilities, they realized that they wanted to give back. They both finished their degrees and are now serving others, Jessica as a nurse treating cancer patients and Patrick as a clinical psychologist. They couldn't change what happened to them, but they found a way to shift how they see the world and found a way to give back.

Our emotional feelings are great indicators of our beliefs and limitations in our thinking. We have the power to overcome the emotional suffering and address the limiting beliefs that keep us stuck. Struggling to complete a project may result in a feeling of frustration, and it may help us identify a belief in inadequacy. Worrying about events in the future may uncover a belief in doubt.

Suffering is an option. It is a choice. When faced with a difficult experience in life, we can choose how we will deal with it.

Here are five steps to take us out of the experience of suffering:

1. Be open to possibilities.

    Resist saying or thinking, "There's nothing I can do about this situation." Be willing to look at other options and avenues. Imagine what a good outcome will look like.

2. Speak with intention.

    Our words are powerful. Speak what you would like to have happen, rather than what you don't want. I add "with ease and grace" to the end of my statement of intention: "I will finish this project with ease and grace. I will meet my deadline easily and effortlessly."

3. Take appropriate action.

    When there is a problem, take action to change your experience. Instead of complaining or feeling like a victim, take action to get what you want.

4. Ask a friend for support.

    It is amazing how often women go out of their way to help another, but when it comes to asking for support for themselves, we become frozen and unable to reach out. Ask for what you need. Reach out to a friend.

5. **Pray.**

    Turning our attention to affirmative prayer is a powerful way to get ourselves out of suffering. How we observe our experiences dictates whether we live in pain and suffering or freedom and power. Turning our awareness to Spirit trains us to look away from the problem and gives us the opportunity to receive. Marianne Williamson states in *The Law of Divine Compensation*: "It is almost amusing when doctors say, 'We've done everything possible. All we can do now is pray,' as though God were simply our last resort, the one we go to when all the really powerful things have failed." Prayer is powerful—it is your authentic voice and has the power to turn fear into faith.

I appreciate the simplicity and profoundness of the Serenity Prayer:

> *God grant me the serenity*
> *to accept the things I cannot change,*
> *the courage to change the things I can,*
> *and the wisdom to know the difference.*

Life can be full of challenges or a wealth of opportunities. How we observe our experiences dictates whether we live in pain and suffering or freedom and power. Turning our awareness to God or our higher power trains us to look away from the problem and gives us the opportunity to receive. This shift does not mean avoiding or denying the challenges we face, but rather it allows us to change our relationship with the challenges. A new perspective enables us to approach challenges with a greater sense of calmness, equanimity, and trust the process of life. We begin to see obstacles as stepping stones toward personal development and opportunity.

Prayer for Peace

I recognize at the center of all life

is a power for good.

I know this day that peace is revealed

in every area of my life.

I surrender any worry or concern I might face.

I release any need I might have to blame or feel guilty.

I release any uncertainty about my

future as well as any fear as a result of my past.

I rest in calm trust and rely on God's

love to bring good into my experience of life.

I live in this very moment, which is filled with good alone.

I am truly grateful for the newness of this day

and the many blessings I receive.

And so it is.

SPIRITUAL PRACTICE

Releasing Emotional Suffering

(1) Recall your most recent encounter with suffering.
- Record the experience in your journal. How can you see this situation differently? Who, if anyone, do you need to forgive?

(2) List five activities you can take to help someone else.
- Add them to your calendar and commit to doing one activity a week. Be sure to record your experience in your journal.

(3) Recite the following healing statement of truth anytime you find yourself stuck in the experience of unworthiness.
- I release my belief that I am a suffering.
  I am empowered with Infinite Peace.
  I am grateful God is gracious.
  I am grateful I am free.

(4) Identify and record in your journal at least three things you are grateful for.

(5) Read the above Prayer for Peace out loud at least once a day for seven days. Feel free to change the words to make it your own.

Download the chapter worksheet at
www.revchristine.com/books.

CHAPTER 6

Money Talks —
Are You Listening?

*There is only one way by which you can
achieve prosperity. It is to take charge of your mind.
You may be looking for some magic formula,
some new metaphysical cliché that will change things.
But if you want to change your life, you will
have to change your thoughts.*

— ERIC BUTTERWORTH,
*SPIRITUAL ECONOMICS: THE PRINCIPLES
AND PROCESS OF TRUE PROSPERITY*

MONEY. WE LOVE IT, WE HATE IT, we need it, we want it. Why does money seem so hard to get, difficult to keep, and so often the source of conflict and upset? The challenge with money is to first realize that we need to understand our relationship to it.

What we think about money is what we think about everything. So if we suffer from a belief in scarcity, scarcity eventually shows up in other areas of our lives.

Understandably, the belief in scarcity doesn't just happen overnight. It is a learned condition. The beliefs

Chapter 6 — Money Talks - Are You Listening?

from our parents and families are handed down through the generations. The awareness of our beliefs allows us the opportunity to update our thinking and make new choices.

> When we were kids, my sister and I looked forward to going downtown to shop with our mother. She was a stay-at-home mom and shopped every Tuesday. Downtown was walking distance from our house and consisted of a couple of clothing stores, a drug store, the dime store, and several small boutiques. She would often take us to eat lunch at a local diner. Sometimes we would even stop at the drugstore and share a root beer float.

> One memory that stands out is when Mom bought new shoes for both of us. When we got home she warned, "Don't tell your father how much I paid for the shoes." She always showed my dad what she purchased, but I noticed that she told him she paid half of what the shoes actually cost. This was a consistent pattern my entire childhood.

> My dad never knew how much anything really cost. He had been sheltered for so many years he had no clue what things cost. Imagine his shock years later when he needed to buy a new pair of boots for himself. He was bewildered to learn the cost of things. In his world, the prices didn't creep up over time. They skyrocketed overnight!

I never questioned my mother's behavior. It seemed normal to me. Guilt, secrecy, and lack were all normal patterns of shopping. The belief that there is not enough shaded every area of my life.

My parents both left high school to work to support their families. The experience of fear and lack never left them, even when they were able to have jobs and earn a living. They did a great job of saving their money and rarely incurred debt, even though their relationship with money was founded on the core belief in scarcity. Every decision was rooted in the understanding that no matter what circumstances changed or how much money they had in the bank, it was never enough.

My parent's fear about money and the lack of money was deeply ingrained in me. While they never discussed money with us, they didn't have to. We could feel their fear and pain. As children, we learn from watching the behaviors of our parents, siblings, and other family members. We unconsciously take on their beliefs and fears.

AFFIRM:
I am making new and updated choices about money each day.

There is a story often told of a woman learning to make a pot roast. Her mother explained the importance of cutting off the ends of the roast before placing it in the pan. The young woman questioned why it was necessary to waste part of the roast. Her mother said, "I was taught by my mother, and that's just the way to cook a roast." Not satisfied with that answer, the young woman, at her next visit with her grandmother, asked why the ends of the pot roast were cut off. "We had to," she replied, "We didn't have a pan big enough for the roast to fit in."

Sometimes the underlying meanings about the perceptions of life that we take for granted become obscured. Unhealthy beliefs about money are the most powerful because they immediately reflect in our lives. In a sense, money talks to us. If it stays away, most likely there is a hidden belief that there is not enough. If it shows up but leaves quickly, the belief is that good things don't last.

One of the most predominant beliefs about money is that there is not enough. The feeling of lack stirs up fear, which raises doubt and keeps us stuck.

Notice that when fear is present, our ideas shrink, opportunities feel diminished, and everything appears limited. When we make choices based on fear, a sense of chaos takes over, and we end up making decisions that aren't in our best interest.

The truth is that there is an abundance of money in the world, and in fact, there is enough to go around for everyone. Our negative beliefs and fears about money only prevent us from seeing the opportunities and possibilities available to us.

It's important to shift our mindset about money from scarcity to abundance. Instead of focusing on what we don't have, we must focus on what we do have and express gratitude for it. When we are grateful for what we have, we attract more abundance into our lives.

Fear certainly stops the flow of good from coming into our lives. The restriction is not limited to money but can also impact our creativity, relationships, and even our self-esteem.

Unworthiness

WOMEN ARE TOLD A LOT OF LIES about money and our worthiness growing up: *Women spend too much money. Women can't manage money. Don't be greedy. Put the needs of others above your own. Don't take risks.* As a result, we often tend to downplay the importance of money in our lives. We sometimes feel guilty about having it and shame about not having it.

Because I felt unworthy, I convinced myself that I did not work for money and that money was not meaningful to me. True to form, the universe showed me that money was not important, nor was it easy to come by in my life.

All the negative beliefs about money take a toll on our self-esteem and our sense of worth. We belief our self-worth is linked to our financial wealth. The opposite is true. Our self-esteem and the value we have for ourselves are the causes of our wealth rather than the result of it. When we fall under the illusion that our wealth is our worthiness, we believe that more money will make us more worthy. When we have it, we are in great shape. However, when we don't have money, we feel diminished.

AFFIRM:
My self-worth is not a reflection
of my bank account.

Consequently, our self-worth gets tied up with money whenever we judge ourselves for how much we earn. It becomes our badge of self-esteem because we believe our worth is dependent on how much we are paid. When asking someone how much they make, most likely the response will be, "I only earn ... ." "Only" puts the qualifier on our income as not enough. Once we focus on what we can't do and what we can't have, limiting obstacles show up. When we make comparisons what others earn, we set the stage for resentment to show up.

> I was employed as executive director of a nonprofit organization. I was happy with my work and salary until I discovered that my friend in a similar position (also female) was being paid more than I was. I became resentful and felt unappreciated. I asked a mentor in the industry for guidance. She helped me identify my accomplishments and achievements. I realized I needed to feel worthy about the work I was doing. I was able to go into my performance review with clarity and confidence. I asked for an increase and received it.

When we compare ourselves to others who achieve what they want in life, we often are frustrated by *their* success and *our* limited expression. We compare our possessions—house, job, and car—to theirs and feel diminished instead of joyful for their success. Over the years, I learned to pay attention to my emotions and shift into what I wanted instead of what I do not want.

The belief in scarcity or the idea that resources are limited and there isn't enough to go around, can be seen in the "glass ceiling" theory, particularly in the context of gender equality in the workplace. Women often face a significant pay gap compared to their male counterparts, even when performing the same job.

As a society, we are slowing waking up to this disparity and beginning to see changes in business and industry. By challenging the belief in scarcity and advocating for gender equality in the workplace, we can break down the barriers that perpetuate the glass ceiling and create a more inclusive and prosperous society.

I enjoy reading about successful women who stepped outside the box. Georgia O'Keeffe, Maya Angelou, and Coco Chanel are just a few examples of women who did not allow the beliefs of society to limit their potential. They created products and services that filled a demand. They joyfully shared their talents and abilities. They knew what they wanted and went after it.

Do you know what you want? Most of the time women don't know or have a hard time articulating our desires. Do I dare ask? What if I don't get it? Do I really deserve to ask for this? Good girls are trained from an early age not to be greedy or want too much. So we don't ask for anything. We often stop ourselves from holding a vision for the future. The lack of vision actually creates an aura of confusion and doubt.

Doubt

DOUBT CREATES CHAOS, and chaos leads to more doubt. We live in doubt when we believe we don't have enough. We don't believe we can wait to save for what we want. We often make purchases to fill a void of sadness, unworthiness, pain.

Doubt breeds limitation. Limitation can lead to the passiveness or inactivity or inertia. The feeling of limitation is so dominant that it can appear easier to simply not do anything. Bills pile up, responsibilities are avoided, and the to-do list grows longer minute-by-minute. By not clearing away the confusion, chaos can take over.

AFFIRM:
I manage and spend my money responsibly.

Doubt shows up in our lives as debt. Doubt that there is enough. Doubt that I am able to do what I need to. Doubt that there is enough time. So we go into debt. I learned this lesson the hard way.

> When I moved to San Diego from the East Coast, I met someone who shared my interests and lifestyle and was excited to be in relationship. Where we differed was in our management of finances. I had money in my savings account and was debt free, while he was in substantial debt. He convinced me to take more chances and expand my prosperity. I fell into the "live for today" lifestyle and racked up unsecured debt. Eventually we went our separate ways. After years of being in a stagnant relationship and in a job where I felt I was getting nowhere, I was afraid to look ahead and plan for my future. I left San Diego and found myself in a new city, with a minimum wage job and nearly $20,000 in debt. It was my wake-up call.

I had to dig down deep to discover what I believed and begin to change my thinking and my behavior. But first I had to tackle my guilt.

Guilt

"FINISH YOUR VEGETABLES; there are poor children in (insert 'third-world country' here) who are starving." The intention most parents have is to create awareness and to teach us not to be wasteful. However, the underlying message has a tendency to breed guilt and shame. Even though we may not understand how eating vegetables at home would help a child in another country, the impact on our consciousness is the same. Taken to the extreme, women become paralyzed with fear that their money decisions may mysteriously take resources away from others.

In particular, as women, we have been trained to consider ourselves last. We make sure everyone else's needs are met before our own. Nurturing and taking care of others is a wonderful gift we give to our families and those we love. The challenge is that we haven't trained ourselves to receive. We resist asking for what we want because of the nagging belief that there are limited resources that will disappear when it comes to our needs being met.

AFFIRM:
I am open and receptive to all that
the universe has to offer.
I know there is more than enough to go around.

We often believe our abundance limits someone else's good. We feel guilty that our success or prosperity will take away from someone else. Consequently, our commitment to share and take care of others kicks into overdrive.

> Rachel, a 40-year-old social service manager, spoke up in class. She was frustrated that there were so many people who did not have enough. She was convinced it was not OK to ask for more or plan for abundance because there were so many people who did not have anything. She felt helpless and confused. Was it OK to practice abundance while others live without?

So many of us can relate to her question. But how is limiting our own resources going to help others in need? As we grow in our awareness and understanding, we have the opportunity to create more expansion for everyone. There are examples of prosperous individuals who have used their wealth to serve others. The Bill and Melinda Gates Foundation provides computers, education, medicine, food, and countless supplies for thousands in need. Warren Buffett and his wife, Astrid Menks, are active philanthropists, donating billions of dollars to educational initiatives and poverty alleviation since the 1960s. Their contributions to the Gates Foundation have also made an impact in global health and development.

The often misquoted scripture, "Money is the root of all evil," has been misdirected over the years. We often equate people who have lots of money with unscrupulous activities. As a result, we feel guilty if we want money, even though we do want it and know we need it to survive.

The actual scripture reads, "The *love* of money is the root of all evil." Money isn't evil. However, when greediness, stinginess, and insatiability for money become more important than our relationships, then money takes on an adversarial role in life.

It could also be said that the *lack* of money is the root of all evil. Lack of money creates fear. But when is there enough? Lack is a subjective idea. I watched as an acquaintance who inherited a million dollars subsequently lived in fear each day of losing her money. It haunted her and kept her from making even the smallest decisions. The amount of money is insignificant when fear takes hold. In *Spiritual Economics*, author Eric Butterworth reminds us, "The goal should not be to make money or acquire things, but to achieve the consciousness through which the substance will flow forth when and as you need it."

Guilt can often put us into avoidance. Rather than face the underlying issue, we operate over the top of it and continue to duplicate the same behavior.

> Felicia had a successful business and hired a bookkeeper to help her keep track of her finances. The bookkeeper embezzled money from her, and as a result, Felicia filed bankruptcy. Things were tough for a couple of years. However, she continued to run her business, but neglected to pay her taxes. After the IRS did an audit, she borrowed money and refinanced her home to pay the back taxes and penalties. Finally, her business picked up, and she had a productive year. However, once more, she neglected to set aside enough money for taxes and again had to borrow at the end of the year.

Felicia had the pattern of the same results showing up over and over again, but she did not have the awareness to stop and find the cause of her money problems. Eventually, she realized she felt guilty whenever she achieved success in her life. As a result, money left her as quickly as it came.

Often the fear of success can keep us from moving forward. Buried deep within the recesses of the mind is the fear of change. *If I am successful, my life will have to change. If I am successful, I will have to give up who I am and become someone else. I will alienate my friends and family if I am thriving.*

AFFIRM:
I recognize that my abundance begins with my consciousness.

We react to fear with accusations and allegations about what might happen if we were to have what we want. Frequently, the idea of success sends us back into feelings of unworthiness and confusion. We become stuck in an endless cycle, unable to move forward. The good news is that we are blessed with spiritual tools and resources.

Spiritual Principle:
My willingness is my worthiness.

OUR SPIRITUAL SELVES are already whole, complete, and perfect. Our spiritual journey is a practice to remember our oneness and wholeness. Each day, with each practice, we peel away the layers of false beliefs to get to the center of our divinity.

Truly the peace, health, and plenty of prosperity come not by chance but in accordance with the laws of prosperous thinking.

— CATHERINE PONDER, *DARE TO PROSPER!*

So many of us would like to move past the pain stage of growth and get into the good stuff. There is no detour around it; we can only move through it. Once we acknowledge our limiting beliefs, we can begin to move through them.

AFFIRM:
I am worthy. I am loved.

Our willingness is our readiness to change how we think about money and how we feel about ourselves. When we believe others are the source of our happiness, money, and opportunities, we are limiting the flow. As we deepen in our spiritual practice and our faith, we begin to recognize that we live in an abundant universe. We open ourselves to a greater expression in the world. When we are willing to take action, when we are willing to take responsibility for ourselves is when we begin to see the shift in our self-worth and our self-esteem. Every step we take toward a goal is an affirmation of opening to greater abundance.

Opening to abundance is as simple as being aware of our breath. Take a moment and deeply inhale and slowly exhale. And again. Oxygen is available and abundant. When we breathe, we receive the gift of life. The best news is that it is free.

The breath helps us understand how important it is to receive. Women are masters at giving but need lots of practice with our ability to receive. When someone pays you a compliment, do you receive it or make an excuse for it? Likewise, when someone offers to pick up the tab for lunch, do you receive it or deny them the opportunity to give? We know how wonderful it feels to give, yet we deny the opportunity to the giver when we refuse to receive. The feminine nature is receptive; however, we have neglected to embrace that part of ourselves.

The law of receptivity states that whatever we give graciously comes back to us multiplied. We don't know where or when it will happen. It is up to us to be receptive and open to receive.

> Jane and I were both transplants to Southern California. She had a family emergency and had to get to Iowa in a hurry. I cashed out $1,000 on my credit card and loaned her the money, with the agreement that she would make the payments. After a few months, Jane became ill and stopped making payments and stopped communicating. I was left with the credit card bill and rising interest.
>
> I could have searched for her and filed a small claims judgment against her. Instead, I forgave her and made the payments myself. Ten years later, as I was preparing to leave for ministerial school, a friend stopped by and thanked me for

how I supported her over the years. She said our friendship had served her in so many ways, and she handed me a check for $1,000. I graciously accepted her gift.

When we are open and receptive, amazing blessings become available to us. When we connect to our spiritual path as part of our daily activity, there is a divine flow of life. Instead of struggling to balance family, work, health, finances, social and spiritual as separate entities, we begin to become aware of the synchronicity of life.

*I am in the flow of life, and I move easily with the flow.
I am radiantly and enthusiastically alive.
I am free from tension, stress and strain and
I go forward in the flow of life unhurried and unworried.*

— ERIC BUTTERWORTH, *IN THE FLOW OF LIFE*

My childhood pattern of scarcity was a painful belief I carried through my life. My way out of scarcity was to turn to my spiritual practice of prayer, meditation, and forgiveness. I set a financial plan to get out of debt and a spiritual plan as well. I disciplined myself with my spending and my thinking. Instead of waiting for a man to come along and free me from my limited lifestyle, I turned my awareness to God instead. It took me six years to pay off my $20,000 debt, and I received so much more in the process.

Here are the steps I learned and practiced to help me move through my belief in scarcity.

Seven Steps
to Shift from Lack to Freedom

1. **Willing to observe old patterns of belief about money.**
   Write down your beliefs as you discover them. Don't judge them. Just observe your thoughts. Once we recognize them, we can begin the process to retrain the mind.

2. **Willing to be in financial integrity.**
   Is your checkbook balanced? Bills paid on time? Do you make regular contributions to charity? Be honest and do an evaluation to assess your financial integrity. Are you afraid to look? Connect with a financial advisor or trusted friend to help take you through the process.

3. **Willing to receive.**
   To attract more abundance into our lives, we need to open ourselves to receiving. This means being open to new ideas, opportunities, and people to help us achieve our goals. When we are open and receptive, we create space for abundance to flow into our lives.

   Consciously practice your ability to receive: a compliment, a gift, a smile. Expand your envelope of receptivity. When you receive, give gracious thanks.

4. **Willing to not judge.**
   The next time you find yourself judging a thought or action, stop and say, "That's not the truth about me. I am a divine expression of love." Be patient. Change takes time.

Resist the need to judge others. We never know what another person is experiencing.

5. Willing to give graciously.
   Focus on giving instead of receiving. Remember the principle: Whatever we give out comes back multiplied. Do you want more love in your life? Express love toward others. Do you want more money? Give to your favorite charity. Tithe to where you receive your spiritual inspiration. Do you want more time? Volunteer. Remember that fear contracts and faith expands. Step out in faith.

6. Willing to forgive.
   The key to moving past guilt, resentment, and jealousy is to forgive ourselves and to forgive others. It is freeing, and it is imperative in expanding our wealth. Make a list of people you have not forgiven. Speak out loud the following affirmation: "I forgive you (include person's name) for any past transgressions. I accept you, and I bless you."

7. Willing to give thanks.
   Every time we are grateful, we expand our receptivity. We can't help but experience love when we are grateful. Living in the presence of love is living in the presence of God. That presence opens us to abundance, harmony, and freedom. Each day, practice writing about what you are grateful for.

In *This Thing Called You*, Ernest Holmes states, "Realizing that all action starts in and is a result of consciousness, prepare your mind to receive the best that life has to offer. Become increasingly aware of the one Presence, the one Life, and the one Spirit, which is God. Drop all sense of lack or limitation from your thought."

Our beliefs and mindset about money play a significant role in our financial well-being. By shifting our mindset from scarcity to abundance, we can attract more opportunities and abundance. By practicing mindfulness and a dedicated daily spiritual practice, we can create financial stability and security for ourselves and our loved ones.

Money is not something to get. It is to be revealed. Your money has a message for you right now. Are you willing to listen?

Prayer for Abundance

I know that there is one power,
one presence, and one source of all good that
is the Creative Process of life itself.
I know this day that
abundance is my experience of life.
I am guided in every activity and in all that I do.
I release any belief that causes
separation, pain, or suffering.
I surrender any thoughts of lack or limitation.
I know I am living in a universe of
divine abundance and that all of my bills are
paid in full and all of my needs met.
I am grateful for the blessings that are mine
this day and every day.

And so it is.

SPIRITUAL PRACTICE

Releasing Lack

(1) Recall your most recent encounter with lack.
   - Record the experience in your journal.
   Be sure to identify how the experience made you feel. Use the Conscious Journaling Technique at the end of Chapter One if you need help writing.

(2) Commit to completing the Seven Steps to Shift from Lack to Freedom at the end of this chapter.
   - Set your financial goals and practice the steps. Record your progress in your journal.

(3) Recite the following healing statement of truth anytime you find yourself stuck in the experience of unworthiness.
   - I release my belief in lack and limitation.
   I accept Infinite Abundance into my life.
   I am grateful I am free.

(4) Identify and record in your journal at least three things you are grateful for.

(5) Read the above Prayer for Abundance out loud at least once a day for seven days. Feel free to change the words to make it your own.

Download the chapter worksheet at
www.revchristine.com/books.

CHAPTER 7

Hanging on May Be Hazardous to Your Health

Setting others free means setting yourself free.

— CATHERINE PONDER,
THE PROSPERING POWER OF LOVE

HAVE YOU EVER TRIED to take away a ball from a dog? The ball is clenched firmly in its jaw, and the dog shakes his head from side to side, refusing to let it go. The dog wants to play, but it won't let go of the ball. We do the same when we hold onto unhealthy relationships, unrewarding jobs, outdated ideas, and bad habits. We want something new in life, but the fear of letting go is bigger than the pain of the situation.

Many of us experience this common phenomenon at some point in our lives. We hold onto things that no longer serve us, just like the dog holding onto the ball. We know we need to let go, but we're afraid of what might happen if we do.

The first step in letting go is acknowledging that the situation isn't working anymore. It may have worked in the past, but things change, and we need to adapt. Holding onto something that doesn't serve us can cause unnecessary stress and pain.

Chapter 7 — Hanging on May Be Hazardous to Your Health

When we find ourselves hanging on, we often discover that our time is spent manipulating, scheming, and plotting to figure out how to make things work better. It can be exhausting and seldom leads to anything new happening.

There are times when we avoid looking at the reality of the situation and blindly hang on. I found myself in exactly that experience.

> I met Brian on a hiking trip. He was fun and outgoing. We started dating and loved our outdoor adventures. About six months into the relationship, I noticed some distancing. One Saturday morning, while we were out running errands, he talked about how stressful his job was and that he didn't think he could devote time to both our relationship and his job. I listened to him and agreed. Of course, he should take care of his job and himself. I would be there for him. I would help him through this difficult time. I was patient while he was working things out with his job and resisted complaining when I didn't hear from him or see him.
>
> Thanksgiving approached and his parents, who lived out of state, were planning to visit. Thanksgiving with his parents was stressful. Things were still awkward between the two of us, but I was certain we could work things out. I went out of my way to be a caring and loving partner. He told me again that his job was demanding and he had little time for me. On Christmas Day, he again repeated what he had been telling me for six weeks. He didn't want to be in relationship any longer. It was over. Now.

I was stunned. I was willing to do whatever it took to make the relationship work. I ignored the signs. I hung on, oblivious to his communication and actions. Brian tried many times in many ways to tell me it was over in a way that would not hurt my feelings. Now he said it directly, and I finally painfully heard his words.

An interesting part of this story is that early on in our relationship, we agreed that if either of us were ever ready to end the relationship and move on, we would tell the other and honor the decision. My difficulty in letting go superseded that agreement. I believed I needed the relationship to sustain me.

AFFIRM:
I willingly release and let go.

We are attached when we only see one answer, one solution, or one outcome and believe that anything else just won't work. We can become attached to wanting a solution that has to look or feel a certain way. Have you ever stayed in an unfulfilling job, waiting for acknowledgement or more money? Have you ever found yourself waiting for your husband, wife, boyfriend, girlfriend, or boss to change to make you happy? We are attached when we hang on, waiting for the one thing that will make us happy or save us from the boredom of our lives.

When we think there is only one answer or solution, we live in denial. Our emotions take over. Our rational thinking takes a vacation. The pitfalls of hanging on are attachment, disappointment, and failure.

Chapter 7 — Hanging on May Be Hazardous to Your Health

Attachment

THE UNDERLYING SECRET to the law of attraction is the pitfall of attachment. When we are deeply and emotionally attached to something, it seems to drift farther and farther away. The perfect job, the loving relationship, or the ideal weight can seem to be light years away. It seems that more we are attached to making something happen, the more difficult it is to achieve and the more control we exhibit.

When we try to control everything around us, we become closed off from the diversity and vibrancy of life. We may have a plan for how we want things to go, but in the process, we shut ourselves off from new ideas and perspectives that could lead us to even greater success.

Not only do we miss out on opportunities to learn and grow, but we also deny others the chance to shine. When we insist on controlling everything, we don't leave room for others to contribute their unique talents and insights.

AFFIRM:
I am open to unlimited opportunities showing up with ease and grace.

Oftentimes, when we're bored with managing ourselves, we turn to managing immediate family and friends. Seeing solutions for others is so much more enjoyable than taking care of our own dilemmas. We try to exert effort and force our loved ones to take our advice and make the changes we think are the best for them. After all, if they just listened to us, their lives would be in such better shape.

> Karl really wanted to see his wife succeed in her art career. He set up a room in the attic for her as a studio, but it was too warm. Karl arranged a corner of the basement for her studio, but it was too damp. He finally got discouraged and gave up. He felt frustrated that she was not developing the potential he saw in her.
>
> Karl did his own inner work to let go of his attachment to her success. As he let go, his wife found her own inspiration. She registered for art classes at a nearby college. She created a class to teach art at the nearby high school. In a short time, her art career took off.

Do we sincerely have the desire to help others accomplish what they want? Or is there a hidden agenda to get them to behave or act in a way that meets our own needs? Until we become aware of our attachment issues, we are sure to be disappointed.

Disappointment

PERCEPTION PLAYS SUCH A BIG part in attachment. We perceive a specific outcome or result that may or may not be realistic. Because our emotions are tied in with the attachment, we are absolutely positive that the outcome we want is the only outcome there is. When we don't get what we want, we feel disappointed.

> One of my first jobs was as the human resources assistant for a large company's regional office.

Chapter 7 — Hanging on May Be Hazardous to Your Health

Paula, my boss, included me in plans to go to Florida for a human resources conference. I was so excited. I rarely got to travel and saw this as an all-expense paid trip to Orlando, away from the deep winter of the Northeast snows.

I rushed out to the mall and found the perfect dress to wear to the banquet. I fantasized about wearing this beautiful summer dress in sunny Florida.

A week before the trip, Paula called me into her office to tell me that there were changes to the company travel plans, and I was not going on the trip. My vacation fantasy and emotional immaturity got the best of me and set me up for disappointment.

The difference between expectancy and expectation is attachment. Expectancy is having faith that good things will develop, while expectation is hoping that what we want will materialize. Faith encourages patience, while hope keeps us waiting.

AFFIRM:
I release feelings of disappointment.
I joyfully look forward to my future.

Expectation comes from the mind, and expectancy comes from the heart. If I let go of attachment, I open up the realm of opportunity. The more attached I am, the more restricted life seems to be. Feeling restricted can make us feel incomplete and that somehow we have failed.

Failure

IF THE HEART LOSES its ability to pump enough blood into the arteries, the result can be heart failure and possible death. If the lungs are unable to circulate oxygen into the blood, the result can be respiratory failure and possible death. It is possible for some individuals to feel so distressed by the potential failure to achieve a goal or to accomplish a task that it feels as if a death has taken place.

Just as the heart and lungs can fail and result in death, a failed relationship can also take a toll on a person's emotional and mental well-being. The fear of being alone or the potential for disappointment can be overwhelming, convincing us to stay in a situation that is unhealthy or unfulfilling. So often in relationships, I've observed that women hang on with the hope that their partner will change. Fear dictates our actions and influences our emotions. The relationship eventually saps whatever energy is left, leaving us powerless.

> It was Amy's third marriage. There were warning signs before the wedding, but she refused to look at them. Her new husband had tremendous anger, was verbally abusive, and made her life miserable. She refused to leave because this would be her third divorce, and she did not want to fail again. When her health and business began to fail, she finally decided to get out.

As women, we live with the fairy tale optimism that everything will get better. We believe we can control the relationship and make our spouse, romantic partner, or business partner change. We become more attached to a fantasy of what could be than the process of living in a dynamic relationship.

Just as with physical health, it's important to prioritize our emotional health and recognize when a relationship is causing more harm than good. Continuing to hold onto something that isn't working can drain us of our energy and leave us feeling powerless. It takes courage to face the truth and let go.

AFFIRM:
I release my belief in failure and trust
my inner guidance.

Spiritual Principle:
To acquire anything in the physical universe, we must relinquish our attachment to it. We must set it free.

WHEN WE FIND OURSELVES with a clenched jaw, clasped fists, rigid neck, or scrunched shoulders, we exhibit the indications that we have an attachment to a condition or person in our lives. Like the dog holding onto the ball, we need to learn to let go of things that no longer serve us. By doing so, we create space for new opportunities and experiences aligned with our goals and values. It's not easy, but it's worth it.

We don't have to give up the intention for what we want but be willing to give up how we go about getting it. In surrendering attachment, there is an extraordinary sense of freedom, an abundance of possibilities, and an awareness of infinite love.

How do we surrender? We practice taking our attention off the need to possess someone or something. Instead, we identify those ideas we want to express in life. I discovered my own experience of surrender in my search for a husband.

> When I was 45, I decided to let go of my dream of ever finding a husband and getting married. I searched everywhere, thought about it all the time, made lists of what I wanted in relationship, and talked endlessly with other women about how difficult it is to find a man. After years of searching and looking, and many failed relationships, I quietly stopped. I canceled my dating service memberships, quit looking over my shoulder in coffee shops, and stopped begging my friends for ideas. Maybe I wasn't lovable or capable of committing to relationship. Perhaps I just wasn't meant to have one. I felt disappointed, devastated, and like a failure at relationships.

> One day I realized that a close friend was upset because I neglected to celebrate her birthday. I was avoiding another friend because of some past resentment. I had stopped meditating and journaling and was neglecting my spiritual practice. I realized that every relationship was important, and I committed to nurturing my friendships and to taking care of myself. I recommitted to my spiritual practice and my connection with God.

> Within six months of my decision to stop looking for a husband and healing the relationships

Chapter 7 — Hanging on May Be Hazardous to Your Health 125

around me, I met my beloved. He came to me and showed up wanting to attend my prayer group. It took me a while to recognize the possibility of relationship with him, since it was no longer a priority for me.

By taking my attention off trying to find a relationship, I put my attention on giving and taking care of the relationships I already had. In doing so, I became a better listener and was more attentive.

The simple shift in attitude and intention changes our body language, mood, perspective, and outlook. A shift in attitude makes us more compassionate and open to possibilities.

In her book, *A Ring of Endless Light*, Madeleine L'Engle reminds us, "It's hard to let go of anything we love. We live in a world which teaches us to clutch. But when we clutch, we're left with a fistful of ashes."

Letting go requires a level of acceptance, adaptability, and trust in the flow of life. It involves acknowledging that holding onto something that no longer serves us or wants to be held by us can be detrimental to our well-being. When we let go of control, we allow the dynamic doors of the universe to open to infinite potential and opportunities.

Breathe. Let go. And remind yourself that this very moment is the only one you know you have for sure.

— OPRAH WINFREY

There is an often-told story told about a man trapped on the roof of his home in a terrible flood, pleading with

God to save him. A lifeboat, a rescue boat, and a helicopter all offered safety, but he refused them all and drowned in the flood. When he got to heaven, he asked God, "Why didn't you save me?" God replied, "I sent two boats and a helicopter. What were you waiting for?"

So often the answer comes but we are not ready for it or ready to receive it. We must train ourselves to become mindful of the activity surrounding us and become ready to receive.

In surrendering, we free ourselves from the constant chatter about what isn't working. We are then open to discover the other possibilities in store for us. We become aware of our divine self when we let go of the suffering from the past and neediness of the future. Learning to live in the moment helps us stay centered in love.

AFFIRM:
I am willing to release and ready to receive.

I believe the most important part of this work is the willingness to forgive, to let go of whatever resentment, disappointment, failure, hurt we may be hanging onto. Forgiveness does not mean that we carry around the baggage of our experience. When we choose not to forgive, the experience we are trying to let go of stays with us.

In *Seat of the Soul*, Gary Zukav writes, "Forgiveness means that you do not hold others responsible for your experiences. An authentically empowered person is one who forgives. Forgiveness is not a moral issue. It is an energy dynamic."

When we don't forgive, we are invested in being right, in being in control. Unforgiveness blocks the creative flow of life and keeps us out of love.

As we let go, we learn to live in the moment. We acknowledge that we don't know what is next and have no control over it. If we let go of our need for control and trust that everything will work out as it should, we open ourselves up to all the possibilities available to us.

When I live in the moment, I allow Love's healing power to take charge. If I can take time in the silence, I return to the extraordinary place of peace and harmony. Instead of planning, changing, and fixing, I allow myself to just be.

Take a few moments and contemplate this meditation from Eric Butterworth:

Let your mind and heart release all that disturbs you.
Let your body be still—and all the frettings
of your body and all that surrounds it;
let the earth and sea and air be still, and heaven itself;
and then think of Spirit as streaming, pouring,
rushing, and shining into you, through you,
and out from you in all directions while you sit quietly.

Prayer for Letting Go

I recognize at the center of all life
is a power for good. I know this day that this good
is God, and God is the presence of love in my life.
I surrender any worry or concern I might face
and release it into the Divine's love.
I am willing to let go of behaviors,
ideas, attachments that no longer serve me.
I release any uncertainty about my future, as well as
any fear as a result of my past.
I rest in calm trust and rely on love to bring good
into my experience of life.
I live in this very moment, which is filled with
good alone. I am truly grateful for the newness of
this day and the many blessings I receive.

And so it is.

SPIRITUAL PRACTICE

Releasing Attachment

(1) Recall your most recent encounter with hanging on.
- Record the experience in your journal.

Be sure to identify how the experience made you feel. Use the Conscious Journaling Technique at the end of Chapter One if you need help writing.

(2) What are you willing to let go of?
- Make a list.

Then describe what your life would be like if the need for attachment were released from your thinking.

(3) Recite the following healing statement of truth anytime you find yourself stuck in the experience of unworthiness.
- I release my belief in hanging on and my need to control.

I accept Divine Grace into my life.

I am grateful I am free.

(4) Identify and record in your journal at least three things you are grateful for.

(5) Read the above Prayer for Letting Go out loud at least once a day for seven days. Feel free to change the words to make it your own.

———•———

Download the chapter worksheet at
www.revchristine.com/books.

CHAPTER 8

You Don't Have to Be Nice to Be Good

*We can stop trying so hard
to win love and power and influence
because on some days we will
have those things and on other days we won't.*

— MARIANNE WILLIAMSON, *A WOMAN'S WORTH*

MOST OF US LIVE WITH AN INTENTION to be good. We do our best to show consideration for others, look out for our neighbors, and be respectful of our planet. We strive to live lives of integrity, honesty, and decent moral behavior. As women, we have been trained that to be good; we also have to be nice.

> As I approached seat 6D on my flight, I smiled and told the gentleman he was sitting in my assigned window seat. He smiled back and said he was sure he was in his assigned seat. I looked again at the diagram on the overhead bin and yes, 6D was the window seat, and it was the one listed on my boarding pass. He started looking

Chapter 8 — You Don't Have to Be Nice to Be Good

for his boarding pass. "Do you mean they gave us the same seat?" he mumbled, as he searched for his boarding pass. The passenger across the aisle spoke up and confirmed that "D" was the window seat. I did not want to hold up the long line of passengers and quickly said, "You know what, it doesn't matter." I hastily stowed my luggage under the seat in front of me and let the line move forward. It was no big deal.

Or was it? Was I just conned into giving away my window seat? Why was I in such a hurry to give it up? I reflected on how many times I didn't speak up when someone got in front of me in line or ignored my request. I remembered times I felt invisible to those around me. One part of me felt that giving up my seat wasn't an issue. It was a short flight, and I had a book to read. Another part of me was livid because I felt manipulated, controlled, disrespected. Was I just trying to be nice?

Webster defines "nice" as pleasing and agreeable. We are being nice when we are being polite, sincere, acknowledging, positive, enthusiastic, and supportive. And it usually produces great results.

Nice becomes a problem when we don't ask for what we want because of what other people might think. As women, we so often give away our power and independence to others in order to be acknowledged and to be liked. We are so dependent on approval that we give away our energy and time to get it. Wanting to be nice, we suppress our rage and walk around like a ticking time bomb.

We all want to be liked, accepted, and included. As a result, we don't always say what we're thinking. We often hold back from telling the whole truth so we don't hurt someone's feelings. We go out of our way to do things for others so they will approve of us. We suppress what we really think. We hold our tongues. We were taught: Little girls are made of sugar and spice and everything nice. We are told to be seen and not heard. Don't argue. Don't yell. Don't jump around so much. Don't talk back. Don't be greedy. Don't get dirty. For goodness sake, just be nice!

In order to be nice, we learned to appease. Webster defines "appease" as mollify, conciliate, pacify, and placate. In others words, appeasing is acquiescing power to keep the peace. I expressed the ultimate appeasement by allowing the other passenger to sit in my assigned seat.

AFFIRM:
I speak up for myself. I claim my own power.

Melody Beattie reminds us, "We can't change others, but we can change ourselves. We don't have to take other people's behaviors personally. If they have no love or approval to give us, it isn't our fault. They may not have any to give anyone, including themselves."

When we appease for the sake of being nice, we've diminished our power and stifled our creativity and given away precious time, all so that others will approve. The pitfalls of being nice are denial, lack of boundaries, and suppression.

Denial

BECAUSE WE ARE TRYING so hard to be nice, we are usually in denial of our emotions and thinking. At first, it can be difficult to recognize the alcoholic husband, abusive boss, or disrespectful child. Oftentimes, we become dependent on the behavior of others to feel alive. When we need to be needed, we overlook someone's abnormal behavior and continue to take care of others so we can feel our self-worth in the world.

> Charlotte had been married to Sam for almost a year. She loved his zest for life, his ability to engage people so easily, and his fun-loving attitude. But when their new baby arrived, Sam seemed to be busy at work all the time. Charlotte didn't want to press about his work or his lack of time at home until she accidentally found the pornography sites he had been linking to every evening. She confronted him about the sites, and he promised he would stop. Being a new wife and mom, she tolerated many lonely nights and busy days taking care of her newborn. A few weeks later, she received an email confirming a purchase of sex toys to someone else's address. He finally admitted to an affair, and a divorce and bitter custody battle for their son took over the next few years of their lives.

We tend to disregard our intuition when we are in denial. Like Charlotte, we may have suspicions but avoid taking action. We often get into a bind by wanting to give the benefit of the doubt and don't ask enough questions. Asking questions and having more information gives us power. Not asking questions keeps us in denial and powerless.

> AFFIRM:
> I am aware, alert, and willing to
> take charge of my life.

The urge to appease and care for others takes up our time and energy, and we fail to identify the warning signs or acknowledge the uncomfortable feelings that take over. We suffer through many issues when we neglect ourselves and our boundaries.

Lack of Boundaries

TRYING TO BE NICE AND MAKE everyone happy is incredibly time consuming. In fact, everyone else's life takes priority over our own. Our own goals and dreams are put on the back burner while we tend to the needs of others. It takes great concentration, intention, and direction to create time for our own goals while we balance being a wife, mother, and caregiver. When we fail to identify our boundaries, we make decisions that can cause pain and suffering.

Sometimes we need to let go in order to allow others to grow strong and develop their own life skills. Helping is a two-edged sword. If we help without an invitation, we feel resentful. If we help with an expectation of acknowledgement, we may experience frustration.

It is wonderful to serve others. I have been so blessed in my life when I have been of service. On the other hand, service becomes martyrdom when we sacrifice our well-being by taking care of others and denying ourselves.

AFFIRM:
I find balance in serving others and taking care of myself.

Knowing when to help can be a challenge. Helping the caterpillar out of its chrysalis is a death sentence for the butterfly. We often think we are helping others when we rush to their assistance. In many cases, unless someone is in danger and needs immediate attention, we shortchange their process by jumping in and trying to fix things. The caterpillar needs to struggle and work its way out of its chrysalis to gain strength and stamina before it can emerge as a butterfly. Human beings sometimes need to struggle to find their voices. Then when they ask for help, we can step in to assist.

When the urge to help someone comes up (in a non-emergency situation), take a moment to stop and breathe and ask your higher self, "What is mine to do?" Sometimes the greatest gift can be listening. When we listen, we allow others to hear their own voice and work through their process.

AFFIRM:
I listen and honor my intuition.

The ability to establish boundaries is essential. The more aware we are of our boundaries of time and space, the greater freedom we have to look within and examine what is ours to do. When doing things out of obligation, expectation, or a need to be loved, we often find ourselves suppressing not only our emotions but our ability to connect with our spiritual self.

Without boundaries, we risk losing our sense of self and becoming overwhelmed by the demands of others. To live a fulfilling life, we must learn to prioritize our own needs and desires and communicate them effectively to those around us. This means setting limits on the amount of time we spend on certain activities or with certain people and respectfully declining requests that do not align with our values or priorities.

Learning to say *no* is essential in establishing boundaries. Unfortunately, when we don't, we may find ourselves not saying anything at all.

Suppression

IT IS SO EASY TO SUPPRESS our feelings and squash our goals. We don't want to rock the boat or make someone else uncomfortable. We don't want to move out of our comfort zone for fear of the unknown. We often deny our own self-worth and suppress our creativity so we can be available for others.

However, suppressing our feelings and goals leads to a life of dissatisfaction and unfulfillment. We must learn to prioritize our own needs and desires and not be afraid to speak up and take action.

AFFIRM:
I share my thoughts, ideas, and emotions with ease and grace.

Suppression works for a while, until we have suppressed for so long that there is no longer room to store all the pent-up feelings. Then we are in for a bigger challenge because the suppression has turned to anger and is seething underneath. Those pent-up feelings have been churning, bubbling, and boiling, and any minute now, they ooze over the top. So we try even harder to be nice, but now it is more difficult because we are afraid that the boiling mass of anger could begin to seep out. Most women fear that if it seeps out and the anger starts, it will never find a stopping point, because we are aware of exactly how long it's been stored and how our intense rage is about to explode.

What we don't realize is that it is already seeping out. It comes out as criticism, as nitpicking and nagging, as slight jabs and pokes. It reveals itself as a sharp tongue, a demand instead of a request, a snapping statement. We've held our suppressed dark feelings at bay as long as we could, protecting others from our anger.

What if we could find a way to say what we want? What if we didn't put what others think about us above our own self-esteem? It would be an amazing experience to honor and respect ourselves, our opinions, and our values.

I recently posed this question to a group of women at a dinner party: If you could have anything that would improve the quality of your life, what would it be? "More time" was the unanimous answer. I asked: What would you do with that time? Lack of time was a symptom for something else. Most of the women did not know how to ask for what they wanted. As a result, they felt guilty about doing something nurturing for themselves.

AFFIRM:
I joyfully take care of myself.

Why is it that when we give to a friend, we are being thoughtful and considerate, but when we do things for ourselves, we often feel guilty? There is often a fear that others will judge us as being selfish, pushy, or demanding. Instead, let's celebrate having an awareness of what we need, owning our own voice, and being clear about what we want.

As women, we are extraordinary at multi-tasking, anticipating what others need before they ask, neglecting our own priorities, as we do for others. But when it comes to asking for what we want, our communication skills suddenly disappear.

> Carrie was operations manager at a small office services company. The computer program they used to record sales of services was difficult to use and ineffective. Carrie knew it but didn't know how to ask for an updated version. She was afraid she would appear to be demanding.

> Allison was hired as the new analyst. She reported to management that the company needed to update their software. Management responded to Allison's suggestion, and she was acknowledged

for protecting the company's bottom line and was eventually promoted.

Carrie was frustrated and angry. She thought it was selfish to ask for what she wanted. It was a painful lesson. Over time, Carrie developed the courage to ask for what she wanted and to speak up when she saw things that could be improved.

Carrie believed she was being selfish and, therefore, suppressed her creativity. We have been trained to believe that anything we might ask for would be self-centered and inconsiderate. Very often, we see a remedy that would benefit others. The feminine nature is to find solutions to problems and to ease pain and suffering. If we have the courage to express our creativity, we would see the benefit to all those around us.

Spiritual Principle:
I always receive what I feel I deserve.

Being nice is often a cover-up for what we really feel about ourselves. We want to be loved, acknowledged, appreciated, treasured, and cherished. But when that little voice inside tells us that we are unworthy, then we change into our superwoman outfit and attempt to show the world that we are nice, capable, reliable, and trustworthy. Trying so hard to appease others, we tend to neglect our own goals and dreams. We end up receiving what we unconsciously believe.

We can be good without denying our goals and dreams. Instead of trying to save the world (our family, neighbors, friends, and coworkers), we let go and allow them to walk their own path, fall down, pick themselves up, and learn to be strong and empowered. Letting go does not mean we are irresponsible. It is the process of surrendering to the power of love.

Treat people as if they were what they ought to be and you help them become what they are capable of being.

— JOHANN WOLFGANG VON GOETHE

We often give up our authenticity to make other people happy. I always ask my clients after they have declared their long list of what they don't want, "What is it that you *do* want?" And the number one answer is, "I don't know." Somewhere along the way, it became not OK to ask for what we want. There is a belief that it is better to suffer than to ask. It's easier to feel guilty than to ask. And of course, we remember all those times we did ask and our request was denied. We made a decision that it is not OK to ask again. Sales professionals are taught that there are more opportunities for *yes* after you get the *no* responses out of the way.

AFFIRM:
I freely and joyfully ask for what I want.

We can learn to set boundaries and not be in such a hurry to give up our own good for the sake of others. It takes patience, as we learn to speak up for ourselves. The passenger in 6D was not the cause of my pain. If I felt empowered, I would be free to speak up and hold my ground, knowing that was my seat. I would speak my truth rather than silence myself.

It is possible to give without relinquishing balance, to ask for what we want without sacrificing harmony, and to be good without depriving our self-worth. Finding the ability to nurture ourselves is essential on our spiritual journey. Nurturing ourselves does not mean we are being selfish, narcissistic, or self-absorbed. Instead, nurturing serves to renew and revitalize. The soul is fed when we spend time in quiet, go for a walk in the forest, take a nap, receive a massage. Nurturing the self brings balance to the body, harmony to our relationships, replenishes our inner resources, and restores our energy.

The human personality struggles for attention. Our spiritual self is complete within itself. As we deepen in our spiritual practice, we enhance our deep inner knowing and are more easily able to release attachments to the outside world. In *This Thing Called You*, Ernest Holmes writes, "You rob no person when you discover your own good. You limit no person when you express a greater degree of livingness. You harm no one by being happy. You hinder no person's evolution when you consciously enter into the kingdom of your good and possess it today."

AFFIRM:
In all I do, I am a reflection of the Divine.

As we nurture and take care of ourselves we expand our spiritual connection, which allows us to deepen our faith and trust our experience in the world.

Instead of trying so hard to be good, let's focus on being authentic by asking for what we want, by taking care of ourselves, by standing up and speaking up. When we are authentic, we are empowered. We set an example for those around us. We step out as leaders.

It is in our feminine nature to receive, and we can begin by being willing. As Buddha said, "You yourself, as much as anyone in the entire universe, deserve your affection and love." Be good to yourself. You are worth it!

Prayer for Recognizing Good

Today, I joyously step into the vitality

and energy of Spirit.

I recognize that Spirit is everywhere and in all things.

As I realize this greater Presence,

I can see infinite potential in every person,

every event, and every idea.

I let go of any need to complain or judge

or separate myself from others.

I accept wisdom as I make conscious decisions.

I accept courage as I step forward into life.

I acknowledge and rejoice

in the graciousness of Spirit, knowing that

as I celebrate It, I am blessed.

I enter this day with a grateful heart and receive

the blessings Love has in store for me.

And so it is.

SPIRITUAL PRACTICE

Releasing the Need to Appease

(1) Recall your most recent encounter with trying to appease.
 - Record the experience in your journal.

 Be sure to identify how the experience made you feel. Use the Conscious Journaling Technique at the end of Chapter One if you need help writing.

(2) What would your life look like if you had more authenticity in your life?
 - Describe what your life would be like if the need to appease were released from your thinking.

(3) Recite the following healing statement of truth anytime you find yourself stuck in the experience of unworthiness.
 - I release my belief in unworthiness and my need to appease.

 I am worthy to receive Divine Love into my life.
 I am grateful I am free.

(4) Identify and record in your journal at least three things you are grateful for.

(5) Read the above Prayer for Recognizing Good out loud at least once a day for seven days. Feel free to change the words to make it your own.

Download the chapter worksheet at
www.revchristine.com/books.

CHAPTER 9

Looking for Love
in All the Wrong Places

> *One is loved because one is loved.*
> *No reason is needed for loving.*
>
> —PAULO COEHLO

OUR NATURE IS to want to be loved. The greatest gift is to be loved unconditionally. The challenge we face is that we often look for love to fill a void—and we want it now. We believe that if someone loves us, they will fill that inner emptiness and make us complete. Romance novels and movies feed the fantasy of romantic love and a happily-ever-after fairytale.

> I was on the great quest. My soulmate was out there, and I was going to find him. I joined a dating service and interviewed potential candidates. I asked—OK—begged my friends to introduce me to any likely prospects. I was on the lookout and went prepared to the grocery store, the coffee house, to church, to lunch, on the chance that I might meet him.

Chapter 9 — Looking for Love in All the Wrong Places

> I read enough magazines to know how to spot him: buying dinner-for-one in the frozen food aisle, drinking coffee alone at the neighborhood hangout, walking his dog at the park, out drinking beer with his friends. I smiled, flirted, and engaged in stimulating conversation whenever possible. I could meet him anywhere, at any time.
>
> I was determined, infatuated, and fixated. I had to find my soulmate. I had to find love. I had to find someone who would bring me a better life and shower me with more glorious love. I just needed to find him. Now.

Before we can receive love, we have to be love. Before we can love someone else, we have to love and respect ourselves. Self-worth is a compilation of a sense of value, worth, and deservedness. When our self-worth is diminished, we have an exaggerated sense of not enough. We give more expecting to get more. The hole is never filled. We become dependent on the approval of others instead of trusting in our inherent Divinity.

AFFIRM:
I am loving and worthy of being loved.

We must become the person we want to meet. I once asked participants at a relationship workshop what qualities they wanted in a man. The list was comprehensive: strong, sensitive, attentive, funny, courageous and gentle. They wanted him to anticipate their every need, read their minds, listen to their feelings, be the breadwinner, acknowledge them with gifts, provide for their future, and take care of the car. Then I asked them if they were willing to *be* those qualities in their relationship. How quickly they backed off.

Marianne Williamson describes the quest this way:

> I used to think that I needed a "powerful man," someone who could protect me from the harshness and evils of the world. What I have come to realize is that the evils of the world that confront me are a reflection of my own internal state, and no one can protect me from my own mind. The powerful man I was looking for would be, foremost, someone who supported me in keeping on track spiritually and in so maintaining clarity within myself that life would pose fewer problems. When it did get rough, he would help me forgive.

The law of reciprocity states: Whatever I give out graciously comes back to me multiplied. If you want to receive more love in your life, give more love in your life. If you want more attention, give attention to others. Love is a two-way street. The more we give the qualities we admire, the more we open ourselves to receive them.

Often women confuse the search for love and the chance to be in love. "In love" is that beginning stage of relationship where everything is new and exciting. We can't stand being apart and find the qualities of our newest soul mate to be charming, funny, and entertaining. We believe our relationship will be this way forever and can't imagine ever being without our beloved.

Chapter 9 — Looking for Love in All the Wrong Places

Actually, the "in love" stage doesn't last long at all. Eventually, we come down from the cloud we were floating on and plant our feet on the ground. Our eyes are open now, and we may begin to see the personality qualities of our new soulmate as irritating, annoying, and, at times, exasperating. Why hasn't he made me happy? The need for others to fill the hole inside leads us to dependency.

Dependency

We are dependent when we rely on someone else, when we feel unable to accomplish something on our own. We want someone else to help us make decisions, to validate who we are in the world. We become dependent on our mates, employers, friends to make us feel whole.

Dependency is a natural human trait. We all rely on others at some point in our lives. Whether it's seeking guidance from our parents as children or asking our friends for advice as adults, we need others to help us navigate life's challenges. However, when we are afraid to make decisions or take action on our own, we can be detrimental to our own well-being and relationships.

We are in a state of dependency when we feel insecure and lack confidence in our abilities. We may seek constant reassurance from others to validate our worth or for approval. The problem with depending on others too much is that it can lead to a sense of powerlessness, making us feel inadequate and vulnerable, which is what Miranda experienced.

Miranda was afraid of making decisions herself. She relied on her husband to tell her what to do and to guide her in her career. She grew to be dependent on him to make her feel good when she was down, to encourage her when she was stuck, and to pick her up when things fell apart. He became an unwilling caretaker and did not appreciate his role. Their marriage was on shaky ground and started to unravel because of her neediness.

Miranda's fear of making decisions kept her powerless. Being dependent on others depletes our self-worth and can alienate those around us. Consciously asking for support is being empowered.

AFFIRM:
I know I am guided and directed each day.
I am empowered to make decisions.

Instead of feeling powerless, we often expend our energy controlling family, friends, and coworkers. We are convinced we know what is best for them. We feel compelled to give them direction and guidance. We take on a codependent role, and while we are sincerely compassionate and willing to help anyone in need, we can neglect our own health and well-being.

Dependency is a trap of wanting others to make us feel better. Codependency is believing we have the answers for others to live productive lives. Both put unrealistic demands on others and cause us emotional pain.

Our spiritual journey is a quest into deepening our awareness of ourselves: our strengths, talents, and abilities. To break the bonds of dependency, we must delve into this inner search and realize the amazing gifts granted to each of us. Until we do, we will always live in fear of loneliness.

Loneliness

LONELINESS IS UNDOUBTEDLY a significant concern in today's world, affecting individuals of all ages and backgrounds. Recent studies indicate that loneliness has reached epidemic levels globally. A variety of factors contribute to its prevalence, including social isolation, limited social support, technological advancements replacing face-to-face interactions, and the breakdown of traditional communities. Life transitions, such as moving to a new city, retirement, or the loss of a loved one, can trigger feelings of loneliness.

For women especially, the fear of loneliness is sometimes so intense, we will give up dreams, ambitions, and talent to cling to a partner rather than take a step out into the world to discover ourselves. Fear of loneliness often forces some to stay in relationships without passion because it feels safe, comfortable, or because they are afraid of rejection or fear they can't have what they want.

Some women turn to relationships with married men, long-distance partnerships, casual sex, and a number of other ways to avoid discovering themselves. Because they have not asked for what they want, their emotions may turn to resentment.

We look for the next relationship, usually repeating the same pattern, and the same unhealed emotions show up again. We often stay in unloving relationships until something happens to make us angry, frustrated, fed up, and we want out. History repeats itself until we heal the inner pain and conflict.

AFFIRM:
I embrace myself with love and compassion.
I am free to be me.

I know some women find being alone painful, while others relish their independence and freedom. Being alone can be an opportunity to build a relationship with our spiritual self. When I moved to a new city, I knew few people and had even fewer distractions, and as a result, I was aware of my thoughts and feelings constantly. When I finally surrendered to hearing the inner chatter, I received a wealth of information about myself. Fortunately, journaling was my regular practice, and I was able to record those priceless thoughts and feelings. Once I discovered my beliefs, I was able to reframe them into supportive affirmations.

As we grow older and begin to lose friends and family, loneliness can be challenging. Joan Chittister reminds us in *The Gift of Years: Growing Older Gracefully*, "If we're lonely, it may be because we have not looked around to see who needs us. A person who is needed—really needed—is never lonely, never isolated, never without purpose in life. All we need to do is to go out and do something. The world is waiting for us with open arms."

Volunteering is a great way to step outside our comfort zone and create new experiences.

If we're afraid of being alone, we tend to rush into the next relationship that comes along. In the process, we neglect ourselves and the opportunity to discover who we are and what is important to us. When we don't get what we want, we feel resentment.

Resentment

RESENTMENT IS LIKE A VIRUS that works its way into our mind and body, eating away at our self-worth. It is not limited to intimate relationships but can happen whenever we find ourselves not living the life we want. It is especially potent when we want others to change.

> After dating Keith a short time, Sandy moved in with him. The in-love stage of their relationship was amazing, and life was grand. One day, the discussion of marriage came up, and Keith said he was not interested. Sandy knew she could change his mind eventually.
>
> The next few years flew by until one day Sandy could hear her biological clock ticking and brought up the subject of having children. No, sorry. He already had a child from his first marriage and was not interested in creating any more. She let it go. Sandy knew she could change his mind eventually.
>
> One day Sandy shared her concern that they were living on credit cards and needed to have a plan for the future. Keith wasn't worried. His

big break was just around the corner. Then money would no longer be an issue. Sandy was convinced that she could get him to change his mind. Eventually.

Sandy's "eventually" turned into six years. She suppressed so much of herself in the relationship, and now she resented him. She mostly resented herself for staying so long and not recognizing that she was miserable.

Keith was not the bad guy. He was happy and content the way life was. He was caring, kind, and supportive. Sandy suppressed her thoughts and feeling so much and for so long that she didn't even recognize them, so how could he?

It is critical in a successful relationship to be able to speak up and ask for what you want. It is necessary to learn how to have the difficult conversations.

One of the obstacles is that even if we communicate, we hang on to resentments from the past. As we let go of old hurts and resentments, we clear the way for love to come in.

AFFIRM:
I release and let go of old ideas, obsolete thinking, and outdated beliefs.

Here are some helpful signs to identify when you are living with resentment: holding a grudge, feeling depressed, avoiding someone, refusing to let go of the past, feeling angry, blaming someone else for current problems, and being envious of another's good fortune.

"I am not good enough" is the belief that often fuels resentment. I am not good enough to ask for what I want and receive it, to have the relationship that supports me, or to have the job that fits my talents and abilities.

This belief keeps us from going after our dreams and asking for what we want. By the time we realize what we have missed, we regret our current circumstances and the only option left is to leave the relationship. But don't leave yet. ...

Spiritual Principle:
Whatever I am grateful for increases, whatever I appreciate grows, and whatever I love expands.

After years of years of hunting and searching for a relationship to save me from the insecurities of my life, I learned it was more important to create my own happiness rather than to expect it to come from a man. No one can fill the emptiness, loneliness, and lack I feel. I must find it within myself.

I know I cannot feel gratitude when I have raging feelings of resentment, separation, and blame. I've trained myself to take a gratitude walk. I get out of the house and walk through the neighborhood or nearby park and take notice of the beauty and abundance around me. I breathe and release. My friend Gail goes to aerobic class, and Judy bikes across town. We each find our own approach to nurture ourselves and lift ourselves up and out of our despair.

Nurturing is how we empower and energize ourselves. Nurturing is an attitude of unconditional love and acceptance. In her book, *Beyond Codependency*, Melody Beattie invites us to ask ourselves what we can do to take care of ourselves. She suggests, "When we hurt, we ask what would help us feel better. When we make a mistake, we tell ourselves that's OK. We tell ourselves we're great and we're special. We tell ourselves we'll always be there for us."

We practice giving thanks for our talents, skills, and abilities as our God-given precious gifts. As we acknowledge them and express gratitude for them, we notice more of them. Try feeling gratitude and anger at the same time. It's not possible. Gratitude lifts us up and gives us an attitude adjustment.

We must *be* love to *find* love. When we feel love, we appreciate the preciousness of life and all that life has to offer. When we acknowledge our authentic self, we recognize life as a gift. When we are in a state of appreciation, we have a greater realization of our connection with our Universal Source and can see the bigger picture of life that moves us into a greater experience of love.

As we become aware of ourselves, our wants, desires, and needs, we can be comfortable with others and willing to achieve intimacy. Beattie describes intimacy as closeness, when our boundaries soften and we are willing to let another in. Intimacy and closeness are difficult to describe—we either know we have it or we don't. It can be an emotional, mental, sexual, spiritual, mystical experience. We can't try to make it happen. It happens when we feel whole and aware of ourselves.

Beattie says that to have intimacy, we need healthy boundaries: "We need to be safe, strong, and nurtured enough to be able to surrender. We need to know we can let down our guard. To momentarily merge with another in the experience we call intimacy, we must be able to emerge again. Otherwise, it is not intimacy and closeness—it is fusion and dependency."

We need a healthy sense of self in order to have that closeness with another.

Love transforms ordinary moments into extraordinary opportunities. Loving someone without wanting or needing anything is the greatest gift we can give. Loving and accepting someone unconditionally is like sending positive ions or invisible vitamins to them. The good thoughts support their well-being without them even knowing. Love blesses the giver and the receiver.

In *The Revealing Word*, author Charles Fillmore writes, "Love is an inner quality that sees good everywhere and in everybody." If I listen to someone's story, make someone smile, or perform a random act of kindness, I've sent love to that person. When they feel love, they will share it with someone in their circle of influence. The experience has a ripple effect, like a stone being tossed in the water. Not only have I sent love to another person, I have expanded the experience for myself.

When I finally took my attention off trying to find love, love found me. I took the time to clean out my old beliefs about men and relationships. I did my inner work to forgive past resentments. I peeled away the layers of ideas and beliefs I had about relationships. I opened my mind and heart to the possibility of sharing my life with another. When I least expected it, love knocked on my door.

God is our love.
There is an instinctive seeking for all things for love.
Love is another name for life.

— EMMA CURTIS HOPKINS

I learned I must be the presence of love to attract love into my life. I tried every other approach and failed. When I finally turned within, love showed up in the most extraordinary way, beyond what I could have ever imagined.

Love is an inside job. It starts with letting go of the pain from the past. Then there is an opening to express love. As we acknowledge and appreciate others, we begin to receive love ourselves. And it is contagious.

Prayer for Divine Love

My heart and mind are open to accept
the Divine Presence of Love.
I know love moves into the very cells of my being,
bringing light, harmony, and peace.
I ask for guidance to willingly let go of any
resentment or disappointment.
I invite the healing presence of love to
wash away any pain or darkness.
It is love that I welcome
and embrace into my life this day.
I enter this day with a grateful heart and receive
the blessings Love has in store for me.

And so it is.

SPIRITUAL PRACTICE

Releasing Dependency and Neediness

(1) Recall your most recent encounter with neediness.
   - Record the experience in your journal.
   Be sure to identify how the experience made you feel. Use the Conscious Journaling Technique at the end of Chapter One if you need help writing.

(2) What are you looking for in a relationship?
   - Describe what your life would be like if neediness and dependency were released from your thinking. What would your relationship look like? Who are you willing to be within the relationship?

(3) Recite the following healing statement of truth anytime you find yourself stuck in the experience of unworthiness.
   - I release my belief in unworthiness.
   I am worthy to receive Divine Love into my life.
   I am grateful I am free.

(4) Identify and record in your journal at least three things you are grateful for.

(5) Read the above Prayer for Divine Love out loud at least once a day for seven days. Feel free to change the words to make it your own.

Download the chapter worksheet at
www.revchristine.com/books.

CHAPTER 10

Living by Faith

Faith stands near.
You know she can do anything.
She can raise your hopes to the highest heaven.
You can choose faith, or you can choose doubt.
Both are near.
One is the reality of life; the other is unreality.
One or the other is chosen
by what you say most vehemently.

— EMMA CURTIS HOPKINS,
SCIENTIFIC CHRISTIAN MENTAL PRACTICE

FAITH: THE FINAL FRONTIER. We may spend time organizing, managing, arranging, coordinating, and controlling our lives. However, the power to move forward comes from faith. Faith is the deep inner knowing that the next step we take will reveal something greater in our world.

> After my husband passed, I sold our home and moved to an apartment until I had some clarity about what to do. Six years later, I started having stirrings about buying a new home. I started cleaning out closets and letting go of things I

Chapter 10 — Living by Faith

no longer needed. I told everyone I was moving. I had no idea where I would go. I just knew I was ready to move. I had faith that the process would unfold. There was a peace about my decision. Every day, I made small decisions that supported my intention to move to a new home.

We have many beliefs in life—those that lift us up and those that cause us to spiral down. There are beliefs that motivate us to take action and beliefs that freeze us into inertia. We transition from a statement of belief to one of faith when we move from opinion to a deep inner conviction of knowing. I had faith that I was ready to move on to something new. Faith is the difference between an experience of hope and an experience of trust. Faith is moving from the head to the heart.

We all believe in something. We believe in a world that is ultimately good and supports us, or we believe in a world of suffering that takes advantage of us. There is an often-told story in the Native American tradition about two wolves. The grandfather explains to his grandson that two wolves fighting within him. The image serves as a metaphor for one's inner sense of conflict. He tells his grandson, "There is a fight going on in me between two wolves. One is evil—he is anger, envy, regret, sorrow, guilt, and resentment. The other embodies positive emotions of joy, love, hope, peace, serenity, kindness, and faith. Both wolves are fighting to the death. This same fight is going on inside of you and all of us." The grandson looks up at his grandfather and asks, "Which one will win?" The grandfather replies, "The one you feed."

We have the opportunity each day to think and speak words of abundance, freedom, and peace or statements of fear, resentment, and lack. We always have a choice. Our power lies in our willingness to listen to our thoughts, emotions, and words.

When we solely rely on external forces to intervene and solve our problems, we limit ourselves and our potential for growth. We become passive observers of our own lives, waiting for something or someone to save us from our suffering. However, true faith encourages us to take ownership of our situations and actively work toward finding solutions.

Most of the time, our faith lies dormant until a crisis happens. We desperately pray to be saved from pain and misery. In fact, beseeching God to give us answers is not an expression of faith; it is more an expression of fear. In faith, we walk through our process knowing that what we need to know or do is provided.

Once you understand that on a higher level your frequency is one with your Creator, everything seems to change.

— PAUL SELIG, *BOOK OF LOVE AND CREATION*

Taking action shows that we have faith in ourselves and in the universal connection that binds all living beings. It demonstrates our belief in the power within us to overcome challenges and navigate through difficult times. Faith is not about praying for miracles to happen. Rather, it is about having the courage to step forward and trust in our own abilities.

Faith is not a switch we can turn on and off whenever we feel like it. It is a constant presence within us, a seed that needs nourishment and care to flourish. By nurturing and cultivating our faith, we deepen our connection to our higher selves and to the Divine.

Cultivating our faith involves practices such as prayer, meditation, and self-reflection. Through these practices, we strengthen our inner voice and intuition, enabling us to make decisions with confidence and conviction. We become more attuned to the signs and synchronicities that guide us on our path.

AFFIRM:
I stand in faith and live and move in joy.

Without faith, we may become bogged down by the stress and uncertainty of the unknown. We may hesitate to take risks or make changes that could lead to growth and progress. However, as we deepen our faith, we can embrace the unknown and trust that each trial and obstacle we face is an opportunity to learn and grow.

What does it take to live from the profound inner knowing of faith? In our fast-paced world, we would love a magic potion that would instantly change our experience or some new technology that would immediately bring more wisdom to daily living. Those things just do not exist. There is, however, the opportunity to deepen our relationship with God through prayer, contemplation, and meditation. Faith is the practice of patience, gratitude, and love.

Patience

IN TODAY'S WORLD we have an urgent relationship with time. We live in an instant-messaging society. We want answers to our questions and responses to our queries immediately, if not sooner.

So many people I meet ask me the same question: "How long will it take to change my circumstance?" The answer: "It takes as long as it takes. In Spirit there is no time."

> I continued to clean out and organize my apartment. When my lease was up, I changed from yearly to month-to-month. Doing that was another step in faith. The rent was higher, and I still did not have a plan. A friend gave me the name of their realtor. But I did not call. I knew I wasn't ready. I trusted that I would be guided when the time was right.

AFFIRM:
I am in the perfect place
at the perfect time.

When I ask someone how they are, nine out of ten will say: *Oh, I'll be better when the month is over. I'll be fine when my project is finished. I'll be great when the election is over. I'll be relieved when it's January 1st.*

That is the challenge. If you experience this, you probably won't be better or happier. Or if you are, the feeling will be fleeting. When we place our faith in the appearances of the world, there will always be something to be upset about. We will turn the page on the calendar, but there will be a new challenge. You will finish everything on your to-do list, only to find there is more to do. There will always be a crisis in Washington and in government. Democracy is messy. That's why it's democracy.

Whenever we place our faith in something that can change without our consent, we always will have our doubts about the future and live in fear. When we place our faith in an organization, company, person, or group, we give away our power. When we stay steadfast in our awareness of the Infinite Invisible, the Absolute Power and Presence, we stay grounded in the presence of love.

Time is relative. Healing may take a day, a year, or a lifetime. Often we are asking the wrong question. We should be asking, "How can I know the Divine more intimately? How can I live in the presence of love?" It takes patience to look away from the appearances of the world and focus on the inner experience of the Divine. When we live in hope, we are waiting for things to get better. When we live in faith, we develop the patience to know we are on the right path and will see the results we want in the world.

It is important to let go of our attachment to time. As the journey unfolds, it can take us to a number of different places we never would have expected. As we move through our challenges, we learn new skills, have new awakenings about ourselves, and discover talents we never noticed before. The practice to strengthen our gifts is gratitude.

Gratitude

The grateful heart draws to itself great things.

— ERIC BUTTERWORTH

GRATITUDE IS A POWERFUL spiritual practice. Gratitude opens our hearts and minds to the abundance that surrounds us. Instead of focusing on what we lack or what is going wrong, we consciously shift our attention to what we have, what is going right, and all the positive experiences and relationships we enjoy. This shift in perspective generates feelings of satisfaction, allowing us to embrace the present moment with gratitude. In turn, the energy of gratitude attracts more positive experiences and opportunities.

Almost any situation can be turned around with an attitude of gratitude. Next time you feel down, start identifying what you are grateful for. Notice what happens in your body. Notice the shift in your thought process.

Marianne Williamson reminds us, "Giving thanks is not just a 'nice thing to do': it's a metaphysical power. By throwing the light of gratitude on what you have now, you literally increase its value in your mind. The universe then reflects that, turning your rags into a gown and taking you to the ball."

> I deepened my practice of gratitude as I continued my preparation for my new home. I was so grateful for my apartment. It supported me over the years while I moved through grief. I blessed each of the buildings as I went for my

morning walks. I was grateful for the process of moving forward.

Finally, one day I felt inspired, picked up the phone, and called the realtor. I told her briefly what I was looking for, my price range, and the locations that were most appealing to me. At the end of our call, she repeated back to me in her own words what I wanted. I felt heard and understood.

Over the next few weeks, we looked at condos in different parts of town. None of them seemed to be a fit, yet each one helped me define what I wanted in a home. One day she called and said there was a condo that just came on the market and that we needed to move quickly to see it. She made an appointment to see it that afternoon. At noon, she received a message that it was sold. She set up an appointment to see it anyway. The condo was everything I wanted: the size, neighborhood, location, and price. But I had a realization. I told her I could not compete with other buyers. With most homes on the market, buyers would come in with thousands of dollars over asking price. I needed to find a home that was not on the market, where I would not have to compete. Again, I had to let go and trust the process.

Practicing gratitude on a regular basis changes us mentally, physically, and spiritually. It helps us get in touch with the good things in life rather than the things we don't want. It helps lower blood pressure, improves our immune system, reduces stress, and supports us in seeing the world in a new way.

AFFIRM:
I am a divine center in the sacred circle of life.

The awareness of gratitude promotes humility, and humility allows us to surrender control and trust in something beyond our individual efforts. Gratitude reminds us that we are not alone in our journey. It enables us to acknowledge the interconnectedness of all beings and the vastness of the universe. We tend to live in a more expansive and open condition of receptivity when we give thanks.

Gratitude is not just for the good things but for all our experiences, positive and negative. Each experience gives us more clarity and wisdom. Every person we meet, every challenge we face offer us a teachable moment. Each one has a wealth of information for us to continue to grow and expand our spiritual consciousness. When we are grateful, we connect with the heart, which opens us to love.

Love

IN *THE REVEALING WORD*, Charles Fillmore defines love as "the power that joins and binds in divine harmony the universe and everything in it; it is the great harmonizing principle known to man." Fillmore is not talking about romantic love or I-can't-live-without-you love, but unconditional love.

When we make a connection with love, we live a kinder, gentler life. We recognize peace when faced with turmoil and goodness in the midst of strife. We have more compassion and less judgment for ourselves and others.

> Two weeks later, my realtor called. A couple was selling their condo in the same location who did not want to put it on the market. They had some health challenges and did not want to deal with staging and showing their home. She set an appointment to see it that day. This condo was even better than the last one we looked at. I loved it.
>
> And now fear kicked in. Could I really have what I wanted? It was more money than I intended to spend. What if I couldn't manage the payments? What if it wasn't right for me? What if...
>
> I had to surrender my fear and turn to love. I had to remember that I live in a divine flow of love. A friend helped me look at my finances. My spiritual mentor got me back on track to manage my fears. OK, I was ready. I made an offer, and it was accepted. Thank you, God. I have a new home.

AFFIRM:
Love surrounds and protects me,
heals and blesses me.

It can be difficult to maintain a balance of love when living in a busy, sometimes chaotic world. That's why taking the time to maintain a spiritual practice is so important. Incorporating meditation, journaling, spiritual reading, and prayer into our daily activities is essential. The practice allows us to take our attention off the activities of the world and turn within, to a quiet, centered existence. In the stillness, we find not only balance but also many answers to the questions we have been asking. I have found when I have balance, I have less stress and am more open to love. The intention to live in love opens us to compassion for others.

I felt ignored by a friend and avoided her for a long time. Months later I heard about serious problems she had with her children. I believed she was ignoring me when in reality she was dealing with much more serious issues. Compassion gave me the ability to release my resentment toward her and forgive myself for judging her.

We experience less judgment, jealousy, and greed when we take the welfare of others into consideration. Feeling compassion and love opens us to the expansiveness of life. We realize the abundance we have, instead of dwelling on the things we don't have. Does love open us to faith, or does faith open us to love?

If you want others to be happy,
practice compassion.
If you want to be happy, practice compassion.

— DALAI LAMA

Spiritual Principle:
Faith is a mental attitude not bound by the past and unlimited in the future.

Most people think faith is something you either have or don't have. But the truth is, faith can be developed through our daily spiritual practice, through mindfulness, through awareness. It is a seed we plant and nurture.

There are three stages of faith: hope, trust, and gratitude.

Hope is the beginning stage of faith. It is a sense of doubtful expectation. We hope something good will happen to us. But underneath are lingering doubts and fears. They are our beliefs. Those doubts and fears produce a form of anxiety called waiting. Waiting for this person, my job, my boss, my spouse...waiting for them to change so things will get better.

Trust is the second stage of faith and brings a sense of inner peace. As we develop our daily spiritual practice, our doubts and fears begin to diminish. We have a greater sense of peace and experience more trust in the creative process of life. Trust is the transitional state between hope and the ultimate outcome of our good.

Rev. Lloyd Strom says, "The anxiety of waiting is replaced by the grace of patience, which is a calm certainty that something good is happening to us in the present moment, despite any appearance to the contrary." Waiting is an activity of fear. Patience is an expression of love.

The third stage of faith is gratitude. Gratitude is the acknowledgement that something good is happening in our lives. Our human response is to feel grateful. Gratitude connects us with love. We feel appreciation, which expands our vibration of love.

> I was still feeling fear about this process, and I believed the home inspection was a way out. My realtor and I met a week later and waited while the home inspector went through his checklist. All was in order. A minor repair here and there was all that was needed. I continued to pray for clarity and wisdom. As my realtor and I left the condo, we were standing in the parking lot. She noticed it first. A hummingbird was hovering over us. It followed us as we walked to our cars. Hummingbirds are spiritual symbols of a positive outcome. They remind us to trust our abilities and not give up. I silently acknowledged this gracious reminder of faith and my oneness with God.

Living in an awareness of gratitude allows us to recognize and value the blessings, opportunities, and joys we encounter daily, both big and small. When we cultivate this state of gratitude, we not only invite positive energy into our lives, but we also establish a connection with something greater than ourselves—grace.

Grace can be understood as an ethereal force that brings blessings, mercy, and divine favor into our lives. It is often associated with a sense of harmony, goodness, and love. By living in an awareness of gratitude, we tap into this higher power, allowing grace to permeate our existence.

Chapter 10 — Living by Faith

AFFIRM:

I am grateful for the unlimited possibilities of my life.

I remember watching friends and acquaintances on their spiritual paths and comparing my progress to theirs. Somehow they had a secret I didn't have. They knew something or were in possession of a secret mantra that helped them through life's challenges. No one has any greater access to God or Truth or Spiritual Principle. The universe is a level playing field. What we do with our faith and abilities is up to us. The secret is daily practice connecting with the Divine.

When we are willing to press through the doubts and fears and speak words of affirmation and faith, we experience more joy. Life can be filled with harmony and love by laying aside our accusations and blame. As we bring light to those places of darkness, we inspire faith where there is fear. In faith, we walk with clarity, confidence, peace, and love. In faith, we are free.

Faith gives us the courage and resilience to face challenges and overcome them. It provides us with a sense of direction and purpose that can guide our decision-making and inspire us to take action toward our goals and dreams. No matter how daunting our circumstances may seem, faith reminds us that there is always hope and a brighter future waiting on the horizon.

Ultimately, faith is not about avoiding pain and misfortune but about finding meaning and purpose in our struggles. It is about trusting that every experience, whether joyful or challenging, serves a greater purpose in our growth and spiritual evolution.

Faith is not a passive act of beseeching a higher power for answers but rather an active journey of seeking solutions and taking ownership of our lives. It is a seed within us that must be nurtured and cultivated. By trusting in ourselves and in the universal connection that binds all life, we can navigate through challenges with faith as our guiding light.

> *When you love you should not say,*
> *"God is in my heart,"*
> *but rather, "I am in the heart of God."*
> *And think not you can direct the course of love,*
> *for love, if it finds you worthy, directs your course.*
>
> — KAHIL GIBRAN

The intention to stay focused and to stay on target is up to us. Many professionals today have a business plan, a list of goals and objectives they want to accomplish. Our spiritual practice is no different. If we can build our faith on good intentions—on God intentions—we will expand our faith and enrich our experience of life.

Faith is the freedom in knowing that whatever I need will be provided, whether it's having the strength to face the day, courage to speak my truth, or help for a loved one. Faith is appreciating every day as a treasure and every experience as a gift.

Ernest Holmes reminds us: "If we will have faith in ourselves, faith in each other, in the Universe and in God, that faith will light the place in which we find ourselves, and by that Light of this faith, we will be able to see that

Chapter 10 — Living by Faith

it is Good. And that Light shed by this faith will light the way for others."

As we move forward in faith, our way is made clear. That clarity serves us and serves others we meet along the way. Then we know we are living our own true authentic spirituality.

Prayer of Gratitude

I give thanks for the wholeness and perfection

of God revealed in my body,

the wisdom that is the gift of my mind,

and eternal love that is the blessing of my soul.

I give thanks for God's grace that

truly blesses me this day.

And so it is.

SPIRITUAL PRACTICE

Expanding Faith and Trust

(1) Recall your most recent encounter with faith.
- Record the experience in your journal.

Be sure to identify how the experience made you feel. Use the Conscious Journaling Technique at the end of Chapter One if you need help writing.

(2) Name an area of your life in which you would like to experience deeper faith.
- Describe what your life would be like if you walked in patience and faith.

(3) Recite the following healing statement of truth anytime you find yourself stuck in the experience of unworthiness.
- I am grateful for my acceptance of faith.
  I am worthy to receive Infinite Love into my life.
  I am grateful I am free.

(4) Identify and record in your journal at least three things you are grateful for.

(5) Read the above Prayer of Gratitude out loud at least once a day for seven days. Feel free to change the words to make it your own.

Download the chapter worksheet at
www.revchristine.com/books.

Chapter Overview

This handy chart provides a quick overview of each chapter. The pitfalls usually align with our emotions which are indicators of what we are believing. Use the chart to take you to the chapter and the Spiritual Practice that will set you free.

CH #	BELIEF	PITFALLS	SPIRITUAL PRINCIPLE
1	observe	• discipline* • patience* • compassion*	Changing my thinking will change my life.
2	judgment	• shame • comparison • need for acknowledgement	Whatever think about I become.
3	doubt	• fear • avoidance • complaining	Where my imagination leads, my reality will follow.
4	victim	• powerlessness • denial • unworthiness	Whatever I take responsibility for I can change.
5	suffering	• blame • guilt • worry	Whatever I put my attention on increases.

* qualities of mastery

Chapter Overview

CH #	BELIEF	PITFALLS	SPIRITUAL PRINCIPLE
6	lack	• unworthiness • doubt • guilt	My willingness is my worthiness.
7	control	• attachment • disappointment • failure	To acquire anything physical, I must give up my attachment to it.
8	appease	• denial • no boundaries • suppression	I receive what I feel I deserve.
9	self-worth	• dependency • loneliness • resentment	Whatever I am grateful for increases; what I appreciate grows; what I love expands.
10	faith	• patience* • gratitude* • love*	Faith is a mental attitude not bound by the past and unlimited in the future.

* qualities of mastery

Study Guide

Women thrive when we grow in spiritual community. Whether it is sharing our deepest fears, greatest joys, most difficult challenges, heartbreak, or grief, we do it best with each other. There is a great gift in relating and sharing with one another.

The most important element of a study group is to create a safe environment. It is essential for participants to know their sharing is held sacred and not repeated outside the group. Visit www.revchristine.com/books to download the Study Guide guidelines and agreements. At this website, participants can also download additional worksheets for each chapter.

Whether you use this Study Guide in a formal setting, as a workshop, or in a small group, I am honored that you picked up this book to serve you on your spiritual journey. I would love to hear your experiences. Please let me know how you have used this material in your practice.

Blessings to you on your sacred journey.

Chapter 1

BECOMING THE OBSERVER

Practicing Mindfulness

- What behaviors push your buttons?
- Name three of your daily disciplines.
- How do you practice patience?
- Name an area of your life where you practice self-compassion.
- What thoughts are you willing to change or let go of?

Chapter 2

WOULD YOU SAY THAT TO YOUR BEST FRIEND

Taking Steps to Greater Self-Acceptance

- Name one or two of your self-defeating statements.
- Can you recall a time you felt shame?
- Name an area of your life where you compare yourself to others.
- Name a recent success you accomplished or something you are proud of.
- Name a limiting belief and the affirming statement you are willing to claim.

Chapter 3

KICK DOUBT OUT!

Transforming Doubt into Action

- Identify something you want to accomplish.
- List the doubts you tell yourself.
- Instead of complaining, what do you want instead?
- Name three actions you can take to move forward.
- Name two people in your village you can turn to for help.

Chapter 4

LEAVE YOUR VICTIM-SELF BEHIND

Evolving from Victim to Victor

- Identify a situation where you have felt powerless.
- What are some of the victim thoughts you tell yourself?
- Name three actions you can take to move forward.
- Who do you need to forgive?
- Finish these sentences:

    I see myself...

    I have courage...

    I am capable of...

Chapter 5

THIS, TOO, SHALL PASS

Moving Out of Suffering

- Identify a situation causing pain in your life.
- Create three statements you can use instead of blame, worry, or guilt.
- Name two action steps you are willing to take today.
- Finish these sentences:

    I am willing...

    I have courage to...

    I am...

- Name someone you can turn to for support.

Chapter 6

MONEY TALKS—ARE YOU LISTENING?

Shifting My Thinking to Worthiness

- Name three beliefs about money you are ready to release.
- Name three things you are willing to receive.
- Name an area of your life where you are willing to give up guilt.
- Name three financial goals for yourself.
- What are you grateful for?

Chapter 7

HANGING ON MAY BE HAZARDOUS
TO YOUR HEALTH

Moving from Attachment to Freedom

- Identify a situation where you are feeling attached and afraid to let go.
- Recall a time you were unwilling to let go.
  What did you learn?
- Identify three steps you can take to move forward.
- Name someone willing to support you.
- Describe how life will be when you let go.

Chapter 8

YOU DON'T HAVE TO BE NICE TO BE GOOD

Releasing the Need to Appease

- Identify a situation where you are trying to appease to be nice. Name your fear. Describe your outcome.
- What are some boundaries you would like to establish for yourself?
- When do you suppress your voice? What do you want instead?
- Identify three steps you can take to move forward.
- Describe how life will be when you allow yourself to be authentic.

Chapter 9

LOOKING FOR LOVE
IN ALL THE WRONG PLACES

Moving from Dependency to Love

- Identify where you look for love from others, rather than acknowledge it in yourself.
- Recall a time you felt dependent on a person or organization.
- Identify resentment you are holding. Are you willing to forgive?
- How do you cope with loneliness?
- Identify three things you appreciate about yourself.

Chapter 10

LIVING BY FAITH

Appreciating My Good

- Name some beliefs you have changed as a result of studying this book.
- Identify some successes you have achieved.
- Describe your current spiritual practice.
- Identify and declare three intentions going forward.
- What are you grateful for?

About the Author

CHRISTINE GREEN finds her inspiration in empowering others to grow beyond their limitations and discover their inner strength and courage. She lives in Portland, Oregon, and is an author, facilitator, speaker, and minister. She has a background in business, education, and a master's degree in religious studies. Christine finds joy in offering seminars, workshops, and retreats that provide participants with tools and practices to expand their awareness and to overcome life's obstacles. Connect with her at www.revchristine.com.